THE
AYN RAND
COMPANION

$2.75
9/6

Ayn Rand in her academic gown for the presentation of a Doctor of Humane Letters (L.H.D.), Lewis and Clark College, October 2, 1963.

The
AYN RAND
Companion

Mimi Reisel Gladstein

GREENWOOD PRESS
Westport, Connecticut
London, England

Library of Congress Cataloging in Publication Data

Gladstein, Mimi Reisel.
  The Ayn Rand companion.

  Bibliography: p.
  Includes index.
  1. Rand, Ayn—Criticism and interpretation. I. Title.
PS3535.A547Z67 1984   813'.52   84-540
ISBN 0-313-25737-X

Copyright © 1984 by Mimi Reisel Gladstein

Library of Congress Catalog Card Number: 84-540
ISBN: 0-313-25737-X

First published in 1984
Paperback edition 1986

Greenwood Press, Inc.
88 Post Road West
Westport, Connecticut 06881

Printed in the United States of America

10 9 8 7 6 5 4 3 2

To Jay
lightning and bedrock

Contents

Illustrations

Acknowledgments

Thanking everyone who deserves one's thanks in the complex process of writing a book is a difficult task. The acknowledgment chapter is usually the last written and unfortunately memory sometimes fails just when we need it the most. If I leave anyone out to whom I owe my thanks, please understand that it is not that I am not grateful but that at this moment my recollection has failed me.

I am indebted to the following individuals and institutions for their valuable help, suggestions, and encouragement in the preparation of this book:

Arthur H. Stickney, former Editor for Research and Professional Books at Greenwood Press, who was the originator of the idea for this book. Arthur not only encouraged me to undertake the project, but was most supportive through some of the difficult initial stages.

Cynthia Harris, present Editor for Reference Books at Greenwood, who took over where Mr. Stickney left off. Her calm, competent professionalism has been invaluable to this project.

John Hendley, whose interest in this project has been unflagging. He not only shared his collection of Objectivist and Libertarian materials, but also read early versions of this manuscript and made editorial suggestions.

Nathaniel Branden, author, lecturer, and head of the Biocentric Institute, for his willingness to discuss Ayn Rand and the early days of Objectivism with me. His openness in discussion and his suggestions for further research provided a necessary impetus at a crucial time in this study.

Barbara Branden, once Ayn Rand's official biographer, soon to be her unofficial biographer, for providing information and materials that greatly enhanced this study, for permission to publish pictures from her personal collection, for carefully checking the accuracy of much of my data, and for her helpful editorial suggestions.

Terry Diamond, Rand collector and researcher extraordinaire, for graciously exchanging bibliographical data with me, for sharing his comprehensive collection of Rand materials, and for painstaking editorial suggestions.

Professor Douglas Den Uyl, co-author of *The Philosophical Thought of Ayn Rand*, for providing me with an advance copy of his and Professor Rasmussen's book.

Helen Bell, Reference Librarian at the University of Texas at El Paso, for her many assistances in locating information and references through her vast knowledge of reference sources and familiarity with computer data bases. Jim Bell, professor at El Paso Community College, for his willingness to share some of his experiences as one who was interested in Objectivism and its implications for subsequent psychological theories.

Alice Gaspar de Alba, graduate student and research assistant, for her help in the summer of 1982.

Professor Larry Johnson, chair of the English Department, University of Texas at El Paso, for providing a research assistant one summer and a course reduction the next summer, so I could devote necessary time to this project. Professor Diana Natalicio, Dean of Liberal Arts, University of Texas at El Paso, for providing time and encouragement during the completion period of this book. To the Mini-Grant Committee for providing funds for research.

Professor David Hall, chair of the Philosophy Department, University of Texas at El Paso, for reading those sections that dealt with his discipline and providing helpful editorial suggestions.

Monica Camarillo and Vidal Oaxaca, for their conscientious assistance in locating and duplicating reference materials. Ann Schultis, Interlibrary Loan Librarian, for her quick processing of ILL requests.

Regina Reisel, my wonderful mother, whose generosity supplied much of the physical equipment that greatly facilitated this work.

Jay S. Gladstein, my understanding husband, who has been supportive, encouraging, and patient, not only while this project was under way, but through all the projects through all the years.

Introduction

The Ayn Rand Companion introduces readers to the writings—fiction and nonfiction—of Ayn Rand (1905–1982). Rand was a Russian émigré who came to this country in 1926 and became one of the foremost proponents of capitalism. By the time she died, her name had become synonymous with rugged individualism and titanic self-assertion. She loved the United States and considered it the most moral country in history. Her great fear was that Americans were losing sight of the American way and succumbing to decadent European philosophies.

As a companion, this study is constructed to serve a variety of purposes. Its primary function is as a resource for both personal and academic research. A number of its initial readers found it not only useful for research but also pleasurable for its ability to recall for them clear images of many of the Rand characters and theories they had enjoyed in the past. *The Companion* is designed to appeal to sundry audiences: (1) readers who have read Rand and are intrigued to know more about the author and her works; (2) students of philosophy who may have been introduced to Objectivism and would like to find out where they can learn more about it and its originator; (3) researchers who are interested in both overview and bibliography; (4) people interested in contemporary culture; (5) the general reader whose interest in Rand was piqued for whatever reason. Rand is a unique personality and the study of her works provides satisfaction for diverse appetites.

The above truth was illustrated for me repeatedly as I worked on this book. Interest in Rand was ubiquitous. Our local newspaper published a review I had written about the latest study of John Steinbeck; I received a number of calls as a result of that review, but none of them were from people interested in Steinbeck. The calls were inspired by the short biographical note which indicated that I was working on a book on Ayn Rand. The calls were not from contemporaries, but from young people with diverse backgrounds: a swimming coach, a philosophy student, a lawyer, a Libertarian activist. They were all hungry for the opportunity to discuss Rand and her works, and pleased to find that they were not alone in their interest. Never, in all my years of reviewing for our local newspapers, have I had strangers call me in response to a review. What struck me as particularly significant was that most of them had not been born when Rand's last novel, *Atlas Shrugged*, was published. A chance remark, in a social setting, that I was writing about Rand brought unsolicited testimonies from casual acquaintances affirming the strong influence she had had on their lives. All this in El Paso, Texas, where her philosophy was never taught.

Her name was universally mispronounced. When I said I was writing about Ayn (which is pronounced to rhyme with *mine* or *pine*) Rand, most people said, "Oh yes, Anne Rand." Or they pronounced the name Ayn as if it rhymed with *main*. However, rare was the individual who didn't know who she was, once we agreed on pronunciation.

Writing about Rand has pitfalls unlike those attendant to most critical endeavors. Rand's theories do not provoke ambivalent responses. If she is not held in awe, she is usually despised. One's academic peers, whose politics are generally left of center, consider her political theories a little to the right of the John Birch Society and they question the wisdom of your choice of subjects. These same individuals would not question the study of Ezra Pound who was a rabid anti-Semite and made treasonous broadcasts for Fascist governments. So much for academic objectivity.

And if Rand's antagonists are suspicious of anyone who is writing about her, Rand and her acknowledged followers are doubly wary. Rand has been attacked so often and so viciously that they are concerned that she be represented fairly. Rand questioned the motives of anyone who was not within the pale. She was particularly watchful that her theories not be appropriated to advance causes she was not in agreement with. Another of her concerns was that her ideas, which she considered her property, not be exploited to the financial benefit of someone else. She was given to litigiousness.[1] She sued a publisher for using her name in the promotional material for a book.[2] While Rand encouraged students, supporters, and friends to study, discuss and disseminate Objectivist ideas, she warned against those who would attempt to act as "spokesmen for Objectivism."[3]

My purpose in this work is to present as unbiased an overview of the Ayn Rand oeuvre as possible; my goal is to contribute to research resources rather than engage in polemics. However, because of the pitfalls mentioned above, I think I should clarify my position vis-à-vis Rand. Obviously, I have more than a passing interest in the subject and would not be writing this book if I did not consider Rand's works significant. However, I am not a spokesperson for Objectivism, nor am I a student of Objectivism if by that one means that one is studying the subject in the hopes of being acknowledged as one of its spokespeople. What I am is an Ayn Rand scholar, in the academic sense. Just as some writers choose to study the works of Ernest Hemingway or F. Scott Fitzgerald and become Hemingway or Fitzgerald scholars, so I have chosen to study the works of Ayn Rand, but would no more think of becoming a follower of Rand than I would choose to follow Hemingway, much as I admire his work.

Ayn Rand can, however, be compared to Hemingway and Fitzgerald in that her public persona came to be as well known and defined as the most carefully created fictional character. Just as the flaming, hell-bent-for-leather, jazz-age johnny became indistinguishable in the public mind from the hard-drinking, fountain-swimming Scott, and the "macho," adventuresome Hemingway hero was outswaggered by "Papa" himself, so Ayn Rand became the quintessential Rand heroine. She presented herself as representative of her fictional ideal: rational, objective, uncompromising, unswerving. Her followers could find no imperfections. This tended to create a situation in which all who were not fully in accord with Rand were seen as being part of the opposition.

Given the above difficulties, I have attempted to remain as objective as possible. I was originally asked to consider this project by a former research editor for Greenwood Press, who, having read my article about Rand published in *College English*, concluded that I could produce the appropriate research guide.[4] When I was being considered to write the Ayn Rand entry for *American Women Writers*, I was carefully screened by Lina Mainero, the editor, and Frederick Ungar, the publisher.[5]

Objectivity does not preclude judgment, however, and on those occasions where evaluation is suitable, I have not hesitated to convey my conclusions. In those cases, I have taken pains to delineate clearly when Rand's works are being summarized and when the opinions are those of the author. Some chapters are naturally more subjective than others. In the chapter on criticism of Rand's works, for example, I consider it appropriate to point out the prejudices of particular reviewers as well as obvious limitations in their approaches. On all occasions where I have paraphrased or represented Rand's views I have attempted to be accurate in matter and tone.

If I were to choose an alternate title for this volume, I would call it *A Guide to the Works of Ayn Rand*. The word "guide" suggests steering, piloting or conducting. It is my hope that this work will serve to conduct readers to the primary sources which are the writing of Rand herself. Even the most ingenious description is no substitute for the thing itself, though it may help one decide whether or not one wishes to investigate the subject further.

The *Companion*'s organization follows a logical heuristic: Who? What? and So what? Who is Ayn Rand? is the question answered partly by the

brief biographical chapter. The main body of this book, however, responds to the question "What has she written?" That is covered in the
chapters on her fiction and her nonfiction, and in the compendium of
characters. It is also part of the rationale for the bibliography. So what?
is the question that calls for critical reaction and that is provided in the
chapter on the criticism. It is also addressed by those sections of the Bibliography that list works by others about Rand. The Appendix provides
a listing of works by authors who were favorably reviewed in Objectivist
publications. That data would be interesting for readers who wish to expand their list of authors *simpatico* to Rand.

NOTES

1. The answer to my request for an interview was a letter from Rand's lawyers threatening to sue me for copyright infringement. This was obviously a
ploy to discourage my project as they had not seen a word I had written. Dr.
William F. O'Neill of the University of Southern California had a similar experience when he was writing *With Charity Toward None*. Rand's lawyers also
threatened to take him to court. O'Neill suspects "that the threat of litigation
is primarily a matter of intimidation." His book was published in 1971 and, to
date, he has not been sued.

2. "Court Upholds Use of Author's Name in Blurb," *Publishers Weekly*, 31
March 1969, p. 35. Rand sued Avon Books for invasion of privacy because
they used her name on the jacket blurb for *Chaos below Heaven* by Eugene
Vale. The blurb, which quoted a review in the *San Francisco Examiner*, compared Rand and Vale. The court ruled against her; the majority opinion was
that when one is a public figure in the literary world, "the right to discuss her
work, to comment on it, to criticize and compare is thrown into the public
domain."

3. "A Statement of Policy: Part 1," *The Objectivist*, June 1968.

4. Letter from Art Stickney, 26 Jan. 1979.

5. Letter from Lina Mainero, 12 May 1977. Ms. Mainero, a senior editor
at Frederick Ungar Publishing Co., Inc., expressed concern about "the nature
of your reaction to Rand's work." Although Ms. Mainero was opposed to Rand's
theories, she had "affectionate feelings" for her as a person and did not want
what she characterized as "vicious and unfair attacks" replicated in the *American Women Writers* volume. Ms. Mainero wished to be assured that I was "still
fairly open-minded about her." I sent her copies of what I had written about
Rand which convinced her of my ability to handle the subject with equanimity.

CHAPTER 1

Biographical Data

Ayn Rand was born Alice Rosenbaum in St. Petersburg, Russia, on February 2, 1905.[1] Her family was nominally Jewish, though there is little evidence that Rand received a traditional religious upbringing. Early in life she developed an antipathy to all religions, which she branded as mysticism. At the age of fourteen, she declared herself an atheist. The family was comfortably fixed and Rand received a good education. She was an outstanding student; her intellectual abilities flowered early. Her recollections about herself begin at the age of two and a half.[2] She could read and write before she entered elementary school.

Before the Communist revolution her family led an affluent existence. They vacationed at country resorts or traveled abroad. It was during one of the family excursions to London that Rand made up her mind to be a writer. She had spent an evening alone in the hotel room, totally taken up with creating adventures for a group of women she had seen on a musical revue advertisement. When she realized that by creating stories for these characters she was doing what writers do, she decided that writing would be her profession. Though she was an outstanding math student and majored in history at the university, she never wavered from her goal. Almost a half century later Rand was to explain that plot was the essential structuring element in her writing. She wrote, "I write—and read—for the sake of the story."[3]

Her father owned a small business in St. Petersburg which was nationalized by the Communist government when Ayn was twelve years old. Life changed drastically for them after that. What had been St. Petersburg became Petrograd and eventually Leningrad. But more changed than a name. Goods became scarce; there were long lines for basic necessities. But more terrible than the material deprivations were the spiritual constrictions of the basic communist philosophy that people should live for the state. For a person of Rand's beliefs, that was a morally repugnant premise.

By her own accounts Rand was a single-minded individualist from early childhood. She was not interested in the same "mindless" activities that delighted her schoolmates. She formed her ideals of human potential early; her first hero was the protagonist of a children's serial adventure story. His name was Cyrus, and the character Kira, in her first novel *We the Living*, bears the feminine equivalent of his name. Cyrus inspired Rand because he was symbolic of man as he could be if he lived for the best that was in him, if he lived to his full potential. When she began to write, she created heroes modeled after Cyrus. As she explained in "The Goal of My Writing," and reiterated on numerous occasions, "The motive and purpose of my writing is *the projection of an ideal man.*"[4]

Her maturity as a child and the childlike wonder she was able to maintain as an adult are but two of the singular qualities of the unusual woman that was Ayn Rand. Bennett Cerf, who readily admits that he could never win an argument with her, recounts the time he bought her a one-dollar bracelet which made her "happy as a child." He compared her to a twelve-year-old girl in the pleasure she could derive from simple things.[5]

Life in Communist Russia was unbearable for the young woman whose notebooks were already full of outlines for the novels she was later to write. But it was not only the Communist government that filled Rand full of hostility toward the country of her birth. There were other features of life in Russia that were anathema to her. During a television interview she characterized Russia as "the ugliest, and incidentally, the most mystical country on earth." When she left it, the primary feeling she had for it was "complete loathing."[6]

Rand left Soviet Russia in 1926. She had graduated from the University of Petrograd two years earlier and had her twenty-first birthday in transit to the United States. The occasion for her leaving was an invitation to visit relatives who lived in Chicago. Rand had always dreamed of America; she considered New York City the greatest city in the world. Its skyline was indicative to her of the wonders that the human mind was capable of creating. Rand accepted the invitation for a visit, but there was never any doubt in her mind that she would not return to live in Russia. The principles upon which the United States was founded—an individual's right to life, liberty, and the pursuit of happiness—were, in Rand's mind, the only proper basis for government. When she arrived in this country she did not know how she would manage it, but she had decided to stay in America.

She did not remain in Chicago for long. Her goal was to become a writer, and as she was not yet accomplished in her new tongue, she decided to try to write for the silent screen. American movies such as *The*

Mark of Zorro and *The Island of Lost Ships* were among her favorite diversions in Russia.[7] In a scene straight out of a Hollywood movie, she met Cecil B. De Mille on her second day in town, after her only lead for work in Hollywood had fizzled. He offered her a job as an extra on the set of his movie *The King of Kings*. There, in a scene worthy of her romantic novels, she met a bit player, the man who was to be her husband and devoted companion until his death, almost three years before her own.

Though there is not much public evidence to corroborate Rand's vaunted opinion of Frank O'Connor, she always characterized him as her "top value." He was a handsome man, a kind man, decent and gentle, but by all evidence unassertive, passive, not at all like the Rand version of an ideal man. Nathaniel Branden, who feels that between 1950 and 1968 he knew Frank O'Connor better than anyone other than Ayn Rand did, describes him as "a very, very passive man . . . not intellectually inclined . . . not motivated by powerful purposes in any sense."[8] Branden expressed great affection for O'Connor as well as the belief that he had much unrealized artistic talent. Rand steadfastly maintained, however, that "every hero was modeled after him."[9] When Charles Francis O'Connor died in 1979 at the age of 82, he was known as the "husband of the writer Ayn Rand." His obituary noted that he had appeared in several motion pictures and been a member of the Art Students League from 1955 to 1966. Rand's unrealistic depiction of her husband is one of the areas in which Rand appears to have contradicted her principle of never faking reality.

Whatever the realities of Frank O'Connor's public persona, in him Ayn Rand found a spiritual soul mate, a man who would be with her in a way no one else was with her, a man who remained devoted and supportive through a fifty-year marriage. Though O'Connor was not articulate about his philosophy in the way that Rand was, he was in agreement with her about basic principles. They were married in 1929.

Success did not come to Ayn Rand early. She worked as an extra and a junior screenwriter, on and off, until Mr. De Mille closed his independent studio. That was in 1928. She then did odd jobs such as waiting tables and stuffing envelopes until she got a position in the wardrobe department of RKO Pictures. Bennett Cerf tells the story of Ayn Rand, some twenty years later, reminding his wife Phyllis Fraser that she had been the one to hand Ms. Fraser her costumes when Fraser was a starlet at RKO.[10] Rand stayed with RKO until 1932, when her first full-length, original screenplay, *Red Pawn*, was sold to Universal Pictures. The screenplay was never made into a movie. She then began doing screenwriting jobs for Universal Pictures, Paramount Pictures, and Metro-Goldwyn-Mayer.[11] On her own time she was working on several projects. Her first play, originally titled *Penthouse Legend*, was renamed *Night of January 16th* when it was produced on Broadway. It was completed in 1933 as was *We the Living*, her first novel.

These first successes established a pattern that was to recur through much of Rand's professional career. Regardless of what pressures were brought to bear, regardless of how many of those in power told her that she must change her style, regardless of what obstacles she found to "doing it her way," Rand remained true to her purposes in writing. Her screenplays were returned to her as improbable; one publishing house after another rejected her novel. Still, when a Broadway producer wanted to buy her play with the standard proviso that he could make changes as necessary, she rejected his offer in favor of a less lucrative offer for a Hollywood production which would not change the character of the play. It was only after the Hollywood production when A. H. Woods renewed his offer to produce the play on Broadway that Rand signed a contract by which she hoped she could retain artistic control. Against her better judgment and because her agent assured her that changes could only be made by mutual consent, Rand signed with Woods and therein began a relationship which Rand was later to refer to as "hell."[12] She and Woods were at constant odds about changes and deletions he wanted to make. Rand calls the resultant product "an incongruous mongrel slapdashed out of contradictory elements."[13] Although the play had a successful run on Broadway, Rand took no pleasure in what she called its mangled corpse. It was not until 1968 when she published what was close to her original version that she was satisfied that her name was appended to her initial vision. In 1936 Rand sued Woods for withholding some of her royalty monies to pay another writer for rewrites. She won her case.[14]

Rand and her husband had moved to New York to await the production of *Night of January 16th*. While she was living in New York, she completed the manuscript of *Anthem*. It was rejected by American publishers; the original printing was by Cassell in England in 1938. Only after Rand had made her name with *The Fountainhead* was an American edition published. In 1946 Pamphleteers, Inc. issued a revised version. Caxton Press published a hardback version in 1953.

In her early philosophic journals Rand explores the ideas she was to expand in *The Fountainhead*. A May 15, 1934, entry contains questions about the nature of freedom and its relationship to her concept of "supreme egoism." She wrote, "What is accomplished if the man attains power and prominence at the cost of this playing down to the masses? It is not *he* that triumphs, it is not his ideas and standards."[15] She went on to explain that she did not consider individuals who were generally regarded as ambitious truly "selfish." The problem, as she saw it, was that most ambitious men of the times achieved success by pandering to the masses and in doing so negated the self, thus becoming, in her words, "selfless." The character of Gail Wynand is the personification of the man who becomes a slave to those he thinks he controls.

In 1934 she wrote in her journal, "I have to study: philosophy, higher mathematics, physics, psychology." Once she had decided that Howard Roark would be an architect, she immersed herself in the study of that subject. She read voraciously throughout 1936 and 1937, and by late 1937 was ready to gain some practical experience. In order to facilitate her exploration of the world of contemporary architecture, she worked, without pay, as a typist in the office of Eli Jacques Kahn, a famous New York architect.

While work on *The Fountainhead* was under way, Rand also completed a stage adaptation of *We the Living* which was called *The Unconquered*. Its Broadway production was not a success. She wrote another play, *Think Twice*, which has been neither produced nor published.

Rand acted on her commitment to capitalism, in 1940, by working for the election of Wendell Willkie. Willkie had characterized himself as a defender of the free enterprise system and in Rand's mind it was important to counter the growing collectivism that Roosevelt represented. It was during this campaign that Rand came to the conclusion that those who called themselves conservatives and supporters of capitalism were often the poorest advocates for what they believed in. In her mind, Willkie's values were betrayed by him and his staff during the course of the election battle.

After the election Rand returned to work as a reader for Paramount Pictures. It was a very difficult period in her life. The funds from *Night of January 16th* had been depleted. *The Fountainhead* had been rejected by publisher after publisher. And then Richard Mealand, a Paramount story editor, recommended the book to Archibald G. Ogden, an editor with the Bobbs-Merrill Company.[16]

The story of the publication of *The Fountainhead* is a dramatic one. Ogden staked his job on it after two readers gave diametrically opposed evaluations of why it would not sell. Ogden's firm stand for publication convinced D. L. Chambers, the head of Bobbs-Merrill, to approve signing a contract with Rand. The contract was signed in December of 1941 with a January 1943 completion deadline.

The Fountainhead was published in May 1943. It was positively reviewed in both the *Saturday Review of Literature* and the *New York Times Book Review*. N. L. Rothman in *Saturday Review* compares it to *Arrowsmith* and calls Rand's novel a work of "remarkable vigor and interest."[17] Lorine Pruette makes analogies between *The Fountainhead* and *The Magic Mountain* or *The Master Builder*. She commends Rand as a "writer of great power," commenting that "Good novels of ideas are rare at any time. This is the only novel of ideas written by an American woman that I can recall."[18]

Rand credits her husband, Frank O'Connor, with providing her the necessary emotional sustenance to complete the book. In her introduction to the Twenty-fifth Anniversary edition of *The Fountainhead*, she calls him "the fuel" for her spirit. The book is dedicated to him, and a reproduction of his painting *Man Also Rises* adorns the cover. Rand also incorporated some of O'Connor's real-life expressions into dialog for her hero and heroine.

Though *The Fountainhead* has become a marvel of the publishing world, it was not an instant best-seller. Like *One Flew over the Cuckoo's Nest*, another underground classic, it grew by word of mouth, developing a popularity that asserted itself slowly on the best-seller lists. To sustain themselves during the period shortly before and after *The Fountainhead*'s publication, Rand took a job as a script reader for Paramount Pictures and her husband worked as a clerk in a cigar store.

The movie sale of the novel marked the change in Rand's financial status. She asked for and got $50,000, which was a substantial price for movie rights in the 1940s. With that financial base, she and her husband were able to afford some luxuries after years of penurious living. Barbara Branden's biographical essay recounts that the first thing Rand purchased after she learned that Warner Brothers had bought the film rights was a mink coat. Thirty-six years later *Look* photographed Rand in a mink coat in Grand Central Station where she had researched railroad operation for *Atlas Shrugged*, her last novel.[19]

Part of Rand's contract with Warner Brothers called for her to write the screen adaptation of her novel and she and her husband decided to return to Hollywood to do so. She finished the script in six months, but it was obviously a very difficult process for her. She was later to say, "It was very painful psychologically and I thought, I will never do it again."[20] In 1979 when it was announced that *Atlas Shrugged* would be adapted for a television mini-series, Stirling Silliphant joined Rand as a co-author. The adaptation was never produced.

When Rand had completed the screenplay of *The Fountainhead*, she signed a contract with Hal Wallis Productions that allowed her six months a year free for her own writing while committing her to the other six months as a contract screenwriter. She remained with Wallis Productions from 1944 through 1949 when the screen version of *The Fountainhead* was released. After 1949 Rand was able to devote herself fulltime to writing and lecturing.[21]

By Rand's account her experience with the filming of *The Fountainhead* was in many ways a repetition of her trials during the production of *Night of January 16th*. When a novelist sells movie rights, she loses control of her work. Even though Rand had been hired to write the screenplay, the studio could and did demand certain changes.[22] Rand argued with all concerned to try to maintain the integrity of her vision, and she was satisfied with the result. The movie script preserves her original theme and meaning. Reviewers, on the other hand, were not impressed with the final product. Neither Gary Cooper, as Howard Roark, nor Patricia Neal, as Dominique Francon, received kind reviews. Some of the same kinds of negative criticisms that were leveled at the book were directed at the movie script: heavy-handed, haranguing, and hectoring.

Though the writer/studio relationship may have been fraught with tensions, accounts of the publisher/studio relationship indicate that both cooperated to a degree hitherto unknown. Rather than issue a popularly priced edition to take advantage of the film's release, Bobbs-Merrill advised book sellers to advertise copies at the standard price. Advertisements for the movie referred to the book and stickers were printed to place on the book jackets, reminding readers of the movie version.[23] While this may be standard practise today it was unusual for its time.

Upon their return to California, Rand and O'Connor purchased a small ranch in Tarzana. A house which had been designed by the talented architect Richard Neutra was part of the property. *House and Garden* featured the house, which looks as if Howard Roark might have designed it, in a 1949 pictorial.[24] While Rand closeted herself writing in a study which opened onto a beautiful patio, Frank O'Connor worked long hours developing the land. He grew flowers for commercial sale and raised peacocks. By all accounts and pictures it was a place of great natural beauty. Unfortunately, Rand was very unhappy in such a setting; since she could not drive, she felt like a prisoner in the San Fernando Valley, away from the city.[25] Although O'Connor was very happy on the ranch, Rand preferred New York City and in 1951 they moved back there, where they remained for the rest of their lives. Frank Lloyd Wright drew preliminary sketches for a home for them to build in the New York countryside, but they never built it, preferring to live in the heart of the city.

While awaiting the production of the movie version of *The Fountainhead*, Rand had begun work on her next novel, a work that was to be the fullest explication of her philosophy, a philosophy which at that point was still unnamed. The project was so ambitious and so all-engrossing that she felt she could no longer divide her time and energies between it and her job for Hal Wallis. She secured her release from that contract and the greater part of the next decade was spent writing *Atlas Shrugged*.

200 Contemporary Authors notes that Rand gave up being a screen writer in 1949 to become a full-time writer and lecturer. However, its record of her significant public lectures does not begin until 1960 when she appeared at Yale, Princeton, and Columbia. During the 1950s, until the publication of *Atlas Shrugged* in 1957, media attention to Rand is scant. A marked increase in media coverage begins in the late 1950s and reaches its apex in the 1960s when Rand, in addition to being an author, became the leader of an intellectual movement. The story of the transition from private person to public persona is the story of one of the most significant relationships in Rand's life.

In 1950 a nineteen-year-old psychology student at UCLA wrote his favorite author a fan letter. Rand, who was not given to letter writing, was so impressed by the perspicacity of the young man's questions that she suggested he make an appointment to speak with her in person. Nathan Blumenthal (he subsequently adopted the name Nathaniel Branden) called Rand and so began an interaction that had profound effect on both their lives. The first printing of *Atlas Shrugged* is dedicated to both Frank O'Connor and Nathaniel Branden; in an afterword Rand describes Branden as her "ideal reader" and "intellectual heir." While her husband could comprehend and empathize with all of her ideas, Branden could articulate them and expand upon them.

Speculation in such matters is intellectually seductive if academically irrelevant. Would Rand have written any more fiction if she had not met Branden? Would she have become the *enfant terrible* of American philosophy? Of course, such questions are unanswerable. We do know that *Atlas Shrugged* was the last novel that Ayn Rand wrote. After 1957 Rand published only works of philosophy. We do know that after its publication Nathaniel Branden began teaching Rand's philosophy and, until their break in 1968, was the chief purveyor of her ideas. In the 1960s Rand became the matrix of a philosophical and cultural movement which became so strong that it was characterized by detractors as both cult and religion. The nucleus of that group was provided by Nathaniel and Barbara Branden.

Barbara Branden (born Weidman), philosophy student *cum* writer, was also attending UCLA in 1950. Mutual interest in *The Fountainhead* was what originally brought Nathaniel and Barbara together when they had met two years earlier in Winnepeg, Canada. After his initial meeting with Rand, Nathaniel requested and was granted permission to bring his friend Barbara, who was also a *Fountainhead* fan, along to meet Rand. Thus began a relationship of great significance in Rand's subsequent career, one by which she was introduced to other individuals whose lives became inextricably bound up with hers.

Many of Rand's earliest close disciples, the group she was to call "the children" or the "class of '43," were friends and relatives of the Brandens.[26] Leonard Peikoff is Barbara Branden's first cousin and it was Barbara who first introduced him to Rand. Elayne Kalberman, who became the first circulation manager for *The Objectivist Newsletter*, is Nathaniel Branden's sister. Her husband Harry Kalberman, a broker, was part of the group. Joan Mitchell and Barbara Branden had been girlhood friends. Mitchell had been married to Alan Greenspan. Her second husband is Allan Blumenthal, a psychiatrist and cousin of Nathaniel Branden.

From its onset the friendship among Ayn Rand, Frank O'Connor, Barbara Branden, and Nathaniel Branden was a strong one. Barbara and Nathaniel made the trip to the ranch regularly and were accorded the singular honor of reading the first chapters of *Atlas Shrugged* as it was being written. After a year and a half of very close association in California, Barbara and Nathaniel moved to New York to continue their studies at New York University. Not long afterwards, Ayn Rand and Frank O'Connor also moved to New York. In 1953 when Barbara and Nathaniel were married, Ayn Rand and Frank O'Connor were their matron of honor and best man.

In New York, with the Brandens as catalyst, a group began forming around Rand. Besides those individuals mentioned above there were other professionals such as writer/journalist, Edith Efron, and Mary Ann Rukavina, an art historian. Robert and Beatrice Hessen, who are now owners of the Palo Alto Book Service, joined the group later. They met with Rand to discuss her philosophy and its application to their various professions. Slowly, Rand began letting all the members of the group read *Atlas Shrugged* in its manuscript form. In those meetings was nurtured the nascent Objectivist movement.

The publication of *Atlas Shrugged* in October of 1957 set the stage for enlarging the circle. Publication of *The Fountainhead* had engendered a stream of fan letters from readers asking questions about the amplification of Rand's ideas. That stream became a flood after the publication of *Atlas Shrugged* and Nathaniel Branden conceived the idea of using the letters as a starting place for the teaching of Ayn Rand's basic philosophical principles. He prepared a twenty-lecture course of study which he called Nathaniel Branden Lectures. "Basic Principles of Objectivism" was taught for the first time in the spring of 1958. What followed was a most unusual success story and the birth of a movement.

With Nathaniel Branden as president and Barbara Branden as everything else, a class of twenty-eight students grew into a burgeoning business. When Nathaniel Branden Lectures became incorporated as Nathaniel Branden Institute a mini-culture was born. Not only the Brandens but other kindred professionals taught courses that were taped and later offered in cities all over the country. NBI had a publication branch which published appropriate essays and monographs and a book service that sold approved books. In conjunction with Ayn Rand, the Brandens inaugurated *The Objectivist Newsletter*. At its zenith NBI sponsored dances, fashion shows, and sports events. There was even an NBI Theatre which showed vintage romantic movies.[27] By the time it disbanded, the Nathaniel Branden Institute, which had once had its office on the Branden's dining room table, occupied a suite in the Empire State Building.

Wedding of Nathaniel and Barbara Branden, New York City, January 10, 1953. Frank O'Connor has his back to the camera. Ayn Rand is matron of honor.

Ayn Rand and Barbara Branden in Barbara Branden's apartment, New York City, in the mid 1960s.

The Nathaniel Branden Institute was a business with a purpose; that purpose was changing the world. And Objectivism was the foundation upon which this new world was to be erected. During the 1960s, Objectivism, which Rand characterized as an intellectual movement, grew phenomenally. Its influence was far-reaching. Besides those who identified themselves as Objectivists or students of Objectivism, there were admirers of Rand, who while taking exception to her close monitoring of her ideas, could still credit her with inspiring them in positive directions. Though she rejected them, many members of the Libertarian movement acknowledge their intellectual debt to her philosophy.

The 1960s were the heyday of Rand's public career. She received a Doctor of Humane Letters at Lewis and Clark College; she lectured at prestigious universities such as Harvard, Massachusetts Institute of Technology, and Johns Hopkins University. She was a regular speaker at the Ford Hall Forum in Boston, she was a *Playboy* interviewee, and bumper stickers displayed *Atlas Shrugged*'s opening question, "Who is John Galt?" Rand conveyed her ideas on her own radio programs, she wrote a newspaper column, edited a newsletter which grew into a journal, and published a number of books on her philosophy. She attracted a large number of followers; her philosophy and following frightened those who opposed her ideas. She was adored; she was reviled.

Rand had never been a social being. The kind of human interaction she enjoyed was intellectual. On a one-to-one basis she was very charismatic. She had the ability to charm even those who were strongly opposed to her ideas. Both Clifton Fadiman and George Axelrod were taken with her.[28] John O'Hara wrote his daughter that Rand, whom he had heard described as a "terror," was "fun, actually."[29] Intellectually, she could best anyone in an argument. Hiram Haydn complains in his autobiography that in his dealings with Rand he always ended up feeling just like her "concept of the softheaded, ambivalent, tortured liberal!"[30] Bennett Cerf concurred, "You can't argue with Ayn Rand. She's so clever at it, she makes a fool out of you."[31]

Another characteristic of Rand's interpersonal relationships was their impermanence. Jerome Tuccille satirizes what he calls her "purges," and recreates fictionalized scenes in which both Leonard Liggio and Murray Rothbard are expunged from Rand's inner circle for their deviationism.[32] Barbara Branden calls these interpersonal ruptures "breaks," and recalls that Rand even broke with the sister she had brought from Russia after nearly a half century's separation.[33] Edith Efron's was one of the earliest excommunications. Rand also broke with Henry Mark Holzer (her lawyer) and with Bennett Cerf. Cerf, who thought Rand a brilliant and remarkable woman, blames what he calls "her sycophants" for her imperious ways. He theorizes that all the adulation made her opinionated, autocratic, and convinced of her omniscience.[34] While those characteristics may have been exacerbated by her place at the head of an intellectual movement, the supreme egoism and the strong convictions were evident long before she became famous.

The most significant break in terms of the effect on both Rand's personal and professional life was in 1968 when Rand repudiated both Nathaniel and Barbara Branden in an *Objectivist* article "To Whom It May Concern." Allan Blumenthal, Alan Greenspan, Leonard Peikoff, and Mary Ann (Rukavina) Sures joined her in the public condemnation and repudiation. The Brandens, who by that time were in the process of a divorce, responded in separate letters "In Answer to Ayn Rand." An important factor in the break was the fact that Branden had developed a serious relationship with Patricia Wynand, which he kept secret from Rand. Besides deception, Rand accused Branden of serious psychoepistemological problems and of profiting from the "gold mine" of her name.[35] The Brandens' responses counter Rand's accusations. Nathaniel Branden hints that the real problem is that he rejected Rand's romantic advances.[36] Barbara Branden, while expressing regret at having to choose between Ayn Rand and the principles Rand taught her, and acknowledging the wrongness of Nathaniel's deception, describes what she sees as the contradictions in Rand's behavior and accusations.[37]

Leonard Peikoff ultimately replaced Nathaniel Branden as Rand's heir. He became associate editor of *The Objectivist* and the main teacher of courses in Objectivism. He was also a contributing editor for *The Ayn Rand Letter*. In more recent years he has been a consulting editor for *The Intellectual Activist* and *The Objectivist Forum*. Peikoff is Rand's literary executor and has announced plans to publish much previously unpublished material.

Though the Objectivist movement was profoundly affected by the rupture which pitted friends and family against each other, Rand's general popularity was largely unaffected. She continued to publish her reactions to contemporary events, her essays were gathered into books and published and she was a much sought-after speaker. In 1974 she was the graduation speaker at West Point. In 1979 NBC announced plans to develop a television mini-series based on *Atlas Shrugged*. Rand fans anxiously awaited its network production.

During the 1970s both Ayn Rand and Frank O'Connor suffered from health problems. The cigarettes that had served Rand effectively as a dramatic symbol served her ill in real life. One lung had to be removed because of cancer. She stopped publishing *The Ayn Rand Letter*, but she continued to write and lecture.

Frank O'Connor died in November of 1979. Rand remained true to her principles. When asked on a Phil Donahue show shortly after her husband's death whether she didn't wish there was an afterlife so she could see him again, she promptly replied, "Oh no, if I believed that I would kill myself right now so I could be with him." She remained alert and active in her later years. Her last speech was in November of 1981 at the conference of the National Committee for Monetary Reform. Though her health was precarious, she was still scheduled to lecture at the Ford Hall Forum the following spring. Leonard Peikoff delivered that speech; Ayn Rand died in her apartment on March 6, 1982.

NOTES

1. I am indebted to Barbara Branden for corroboration of the essential facts of Rand's life. Ms. Branden, who wrote Rand's only authorized biography, *Who Is Ayn Rand?*, is currently writing an independent biography, sections of which she has read publicly.

2. Appearance, "Tomorrow," NBC Television, 2 July 1979.

3. Ayn Rand, "The Goal of My Writing," in *The Romantic Manifesto* (New York: The World Publishing Company, 1969), p. 162.

4. Ibid., p. 161.

5. Bennett Cerf, *At Random* (New York: Random House, 1977), p. 252.

6. Appearance, "Donahue," WGN-TV, Chicago, Illinois, 29 April 1980.

7. Barbara Branden, "Who Is Ayn Rand?" in Nathaniel Branden and Barbara Branden, *Who Is Ayn Rand?* (New York: Paperback Library, 1964), p. 135.

8. Personal interview with Nathaniel Branden, Beverly Hills, California, 12 Oct. 1981.

9. Quoted in *New York Times* obituary, 12 Nov. 1979.

10. Cerf, p. 252.

11. *200 Contemporary Authors* (Detroit: The Gale Research Company, 1969), p. 225.

12. Introduction, *Night of January 16th* (New York: New American Library, 1968), p. 8.

13. Ibid.

14. "Author Wins Royalty Row," *New York Times*, 11 Feb. 1936, p. 19.

15. "From Ayn Rand's Unpublished Writings: Philosophical Journal," *The Objectivist Forum*, August 1983, p. 5.

16. B. Branden, p. 160.

17. N. L. Rothman, "H. Roark, Architect," review of *The Fountainhead*, *Saturday Review of Literature*, 29 May 1943, p. 31.

18. Lorine Pruette, "Battle Against Evil," review of *The Fountainhead*, *New York Times Book Review*, 1 May 1943, p. 7.

19. "Ayn Rand Returns," *Look*, 14 May 1979, p. 72.

20. Ibid.

21. *200 Contemporary Authors*, p. 225.

22. Kevin McGann, "Ayn Rand in the Stockyard of the Spirit," in *The Modern American Novel and the Movies*, ed. Gerald Peary and Roger Shatzkin (New York: Frederick Ungar Publishing Co., 1978), p. 328. McGann feels that Rand's script compromises the integrity of Dominique's character and panders to middle-class mores in two significant ways: Dominique does not marry Peter, and

her adultery and its public acknowledgment are avoided by having Wynand commit suicide.

23. Paul S. Nathan, "Books into Films," *Publishers Weekly*, 11 June 1949, p. 2405.

24. "A Steel House with a Suave Finish," *House and Garden*, August 1949, pp. 54–57.

25. Personal interview with Barbara Branden, Los Angeles, California, 9 Nov. 1981.

26. Lewis Nichols, "Class of '43," *New York Times*, 22 Dec. 1957, sec. 7, p. 8.

27. B. Branden, interview.

28. Cerf, p. 250.

29. Finis Farr, *O'Hara: A Biography* (Boston: Little, Brown and Company, 1973), p. 262.

30. Hiram Haydn, *Words and Faces* (New York: Harcourt Brace Jovanovich, 1974), p. 261.

31. Cerf, p. 251.

32. Jerome Tuccille, *It Usually Begins with Ayn Rand* (New York: Stein and Day, 1972), pp. 27–33.

33. B. Branden, interview.

34. Cerf, p. 251.

35. Ayn Rand, "To Whom It May Concern," *The Objectivist* 7, no. 5 (May 1968): 1–8.

36. Nathaniel Branden, "In Answer to Ayn Rand," mailing to subscribers to *The Objectivist*, October 1968.

37. Barbara Branden, "In Answer to Ayn Rand," mailing to subscribers to *The Objectivist*, October 1968.

CHAPTER 2

The Fiction

Although Ayn Rand became known as a philosopher whose ideas influenced people as diverse as politicians and tennis superstars, she was initially a writer of fiction. It was through her fiction that her ideas were first disseminated and it is still through her works of fiction that the majority of readers are introduced to her essential concepts. Though many literate individuals would recognize such titles as *The Romantic Manifesto* or *The Virtue of Selfishness,* by far the greater number of readers are familiar with Rand's novels: *Anthem, The Fountainhead,* or *Atlas Shrugged.* The latter titles are all still in print in hardcover as well as in paperback. The nonfiction works, while still immensely popular, do not compare in sales to the fiction.

Rand's fiction is her foremost achievement. It has made her a world-class author. It is the medium through which her message is most widely and most palatably broadcast. Even those who oppose her politically and philosophically acknowledge the impact of her fiction.

Though she has not published much in comparison to other writers of similar popularity, what she has written continues to sell remarkably well. Her popularity transcends the generations. The sales figures continue to be a publishing phenomenon.

Rand published four novels and one play and one short story. For the purposes of this study, the play will be discussed with the works of fiction. The basic elements of fiction such as plot, character, and theme pertain to both genres.

Rand's major literary works follow similar plot patterns. In each, an exceptionally able and individualistic protagonist battles the forces of collectivism and mediocrity which are threatening or have destroyed a nation or the world. Though Rand personally became more pessimistic about the prospects for individualism in the real world (in 1975 she ceased publishing her newsletter with the announcement that the state of culture was so low, and so many of the dire events that she had predicted had occurred, that to continue to write about and warn of them would be redundant), in her fictional worlds the plot structures become, chronologically, more optimistic. Of course, she quit writing fiction in 1957, nearly a generation before she stopped publishing her newsletter.

Her initial works hold out little hope. In her first published work, *Night of January 16th*, the outcome for the protagonist is dubious. There is a new jury for each performance and Karen Andre's fate hangs on the "sense of life" of a different dozen jurors nightly. Whether or not she is convicted, her main value in life, Bjorn Faulkner, is dead. *We the Living*, begun earlier but published later, has a very depressing ending. Of the three major characters, two die and the third is on his way to sure self-destruction. It is not until *Anthem* that the worthwhile people begin winning. At the end of that novelette, though the world is still in a benighted state, the young Edenic couple have escaped and are ready to establish a refuge for others of their ilk, thereby holding forth hope for the future. *The Fountainhead* paints a roseate picture. Not only does Howard Roark prosper, but Dominique, who had been convinced that the world would destroy anyone with his integrity, has changed her mind and has become his wife. The most optimistic ending is reserved for *Atlas Shrugged*. Although Roark succeeds in *The Fountainhead*, the Ellsworth Tooheys of the world are still solidly in place. In *Atlas Shrugged*, however, the strike of the "men of the mind" vanquishes the looters, leeches, and "second-handers," leaving the world firmly in the hands of the creative and the productive.

A character-by-character analysis is provided in Chapter 3. Some general commentary should suffice here. Of Rand's five protagonists, three are women and two are men. However, the great preponderance of her other characters, major and minor, is male. Her main female characters share certain characteristics: they have slender physiques, defiant stances, and inner calm. The major male characters have distinctive coloring and bearing: John Galt's hair is chestnut-brown and his eyes are deep grey in a face that reflects no pain, fear, or guilt; Francisco d'Anconia has black hair, blue eyes, and lots of style; Howard Roark's hair is a startling orange and his eyes are grey; Andrei Taganov's face carries a battle scar and projects the look of a caged tiger. Grey eyes predominate as do supple and hard physiques. Rand's heroes are all tall, straight, and strong. As with their feminine counterparts, defiance is a keystone of their characters. Fear is never part of their demeanor. Dominance is reinforced with whip imagery: Bjorn Faulkner treats Karen as if she were an animal he was trying to break; Leo Kovalensky is described as being born to carry a whip.

Rand also uses a technique, traditional in comedy and allegory, by which characters' names are indicators of their personalities. Such names as Wesley Mouch, Ellsworth Monkton Toohey, Homer Slottern, and Balph Eubank carry strong suggestions of their wearers' offensive natures. There are, to be sure, many villains with neutral names such as Robert Stadler or James Taggart. However, even if the character has a handsome physical appearance and a neutral name, the reader is never left in doubt about Rand's attitude toward him or her. Ambiguous characters are extremely rare in Rand's writing. The author/narrator, who is most definitely subjective, communicates quite clearly whether a character is to be viewed positively or negatively. Rand's usual method of character introduction is a brief biographical sketch in which the individual's virtues or vices are clearly delineated. Though Pavel Syerov is described as nice-looking, if a bit of a dandy, the reader is quickly informed that while he represents himself as a revolutionary hero, in fact, "Pavlusha" stayed home with a cold during the initial forays of the revolution. Lillian Rearden, whose classic beauty fools Hank into thinking she is someone to strive for, turns empty eyes and a superficial gaiety on those who encounter her. Although she claims to love her husband, she does not value what he does or appreciate his abilities.

Instant recognition of the like-minded is an ability shared by Rand's heroes and villains alike. Though Kira has never seen Leo before, she is willing to let him believe she is a prostitute rather than let him go out of her life. Equality 7–2521 and Liberty 5–3000 need only eye contact to establish a bond strong enough to make them defy their collectivist society. After minimal conversation, she is sure enough of him to follow him into the Uncharted Forest. In two of Rand's stories, the first meeting of hero and heroine is accompanied by a rape-like encounter, which, rather than distancing the couple, cements the relationship. Howard Roark's rape of Dominique establishes an unspoken bond as neither speaks during the entire episode. Bjorn Faulkner rapes Karen Andre when she comes for a job interview and she remains his business partner and mistress for the rest of his life. John Galt's first sexual experience with Dagny is a ritualized rape in the tunnels of Taggart Transcontinental. For Rand these romanticized rapes are symbolic of the head-on clash of two strong personalities. The rapist is conquered just as his victim is. A readership with a raised consciousness about the nature of rape might find this symbolism unpalatable.

When Rand's characters love, they love without reservation. Since for Rand the emotion of love is a response to values, then the object of one's love is a representation of all that one holds dear; therefore, just as a Rand character does battle for that which he or she values, so a Rand character will do anything for the loved one. This is demonstrated in each of Rand's works of fiction. In *The Night of January 16th* Karen Andre is willing to do anything for Bjorn Faulkner. She defies the law, engages in criminal acts, and even allows Bjorn to marry Nancy Whitfield since that is what Bjorn thinks is necessary to buttress his failing financial empire. She allows herself to be tried for his murder because she thinks that she is helping him engineer a fake suicide. "Guts" Regan is also willing to help Andre and Faulkner stage the fake suicide. His reason is that he loves Karen; he loves her so much that he would help her run off with the man she loves after she has turned down his advances. As he explains to the district attorney, even a lowlife gangster such as he can be moved to nobility when "something passes us to which one kneels."

Leo's health is so important to Kira that she becomes Andrei's mistress so that she will have the money to send Leo to a sanatorium in the Crimea. Prior to that she has risked her life attempting to escape with Leo, although she doesn't even know his name. Kira, who never lies, lies to both Andrei and Leo in order to save Leo's life and pride. She pretends that she loves Andrei and she lies to Leo about where she gets money.

Roark, who is fiercely independent, openly acknowledges to Dominique how much she controls him. When she attempts to play power games with him, he shows her immediately that she owns him—"all . . . that can be owned." His love for her is so great that he will not ask her to be his wife because he knows that she cannot be whole until she comes to him with a healthy ego. He stands by when she marries first Peter Keating and then Gail Wynand, enduring the pain while she goes through her perverse penance.

Gail Wynand explains to Dominique that "love is exception-making." He has broken every person of supposed integrity that he can find in order to prove his power, but he doesn't want to break her, although he tells her that she is in love with integrity and in his eyes is a person who has it, a "person who matches inside and out."

John Galt puts his life in danger in order to be with Dagny. Eventually his association with her results in his capture and torture. Before the government agents arrive he tells her that he does not regret her action. Dagny exclaims, "I didn't care whether either one of us lived afterwards, just to see you this once!" The life-worshipping Galt tells Dagny that he will kill himself rather than allow her to be tortured.

Rand's vision of the world was set when she was very young. She had a very clear sense of the kind of individual she admired and the kind of person she wanted to be. Once she had set her goals, she worked toward them with unswerving determination and integrity. She did not compromise her values. She was determined to do it her way. As she strove to understand why people were beset by the problems they were beset by, she developed a set of principles by which she judged individuals and events. Though there are reasons to believe that she was not unswervingly consistent in her application of her own principles, she claimed that she was. The first sentence of the Afterword to *Atlas Shrugged* reads, "My personal life . . . is a postscript to my novels; it consists of the sentence: '*And I mean it!*' "

A detailed working out of all of Rand's major themes would occupy an entire book; after she stopped writing fiction, Rand published seven works of nonfiction in which she did just that. This chapter will focus *only* on the literary works and on some of the implications of Rand's predominant message that can be inferred from the actions and words of Rand's fictional spokespersons.

The major theme of Rand's fiction is the primacy of the individual. The unique and precious individual human life is the standard by which good is judged. That which sustains and enriches life is good; that which negates and impoverishes the individual's pursuit of happiness is evil. All of the secondary themes in Rand's fiction develop as the logical consequence of her major theme. If the individual human life is the standard by which good is judged, then it follows that political, economic and ethical systems and institutions which encourage and protect individual freedom and happiness are the proper systems to develop and sustain. While her major theme is explicitly developed in all of her novels, it is not until *Atlas Shrugged* that she works out all of the political, economic, and metaphysical implications of that theme.

Rand repeatedly articulated her respect for America's Founding Fathers and the premises upon which this country was based. If there is a phrase in the Constitution which synthesizes Rand's philosophy, it is the statement that each individual is endowed with certain inalienable rights: the rights to life, liberty and the pursuit of happiness. As Rand worked out her interpretation of what those rights entailed she saw three areas of conflict in which those rights were held in the balance.

THE THREE ANTIPODES

Individualism versus Collectivism
Egoism versus Altruism
Reason versus Mysticism

In Rand's philosophy all of these areas are interconnected. Reason is the tool by which the individual discerns that which is life-sustaining and ego-nourishing. Collectivism, altruism, and mysticism all work against individual freedom, a healthy ego, and rationality.

In all of Rand's works, the individual human is the most important being in the universe. Not God, nor country, nor cause, precedes the individual in Rand's hierarchy of values. In her first novel, *We the Living*, she pointedly illustrates how putting one's state or political cause above the self is detrimental to human happiness and ultimately creates a destructive and poorly functioning state.

The value that Rand places on the individual is clearly seen in Kira's affection for Andrei. Though she hates Communists, she sees Andrei's worth as an individual and worries about him, expressing fear for his safety when he fights rebellious farmers.

Whitfield, the villainous banker who kills Bjorn Faulkner, states his credo on the witness stand, "I believe in one's duty above all; Bjorn Faulkner believed in nothing but his own pleasure." One of Rand's favorite techniques is this kind of dramatic irony whereby the speaker, in trying to explain what is wrong with a character by his standards, is explaining what is right with that character by Rand's standards.

The Fountainhead is Rand's fullest explication of the primacy of the individual. One of her stated purposes in writing it was to develop a defense of egoism, which Rand has also called selfishness and rational self-interest. Howard Roark explains the virtue of selfishness in his defense at the Cortlandt trial. In his explanation of how independent creators have benefited humankind he says, "The creators were not selfless. It is the whole secret to their power—that it was self-sufficient, self-motivated, self-generated." He goes on to explain that only by living for oneself can one accomplish those things which are the crown of human achievement. The mind, in which great creations are conceived, is an individual thing. "There is no such thing as a collective brain."

The much-quoted rule of living of Mulligan's Valley—the utopia of *Atlas Shrugged*—is another of the specific articulations of Rand's belief in the primacy of the individual. Carved in granite on the door to the structure which holds the motor, product of one mind, that could power the world is the oath: "I swear by my life and my love of it that I will never live for the sake of another man, nor ask another man to live for mine."

Parallel to Rand's development of the dichotomy of the individual versus the collective is her working out of the analogous situation of the productive versus the parasitical. In Rand's fictional world, the elite are the able, the doers. The ability to create, to produce, to do is a primary virtue. For Rand, you are what you do.

This is not as evident in her early works as it was to become in the novels that were the hallmarks of her philosophy. Bjorn Faulkner has a great financial empire, but it is not clear that this is as much a result of his productive capabilities as it is of his financial manipulations and wheeler-dealering. His callous appropriation of his stockholders' funds for his own purposes is more appropriate to those that Rand was later to describe as "looters" than the kind of scrupulous achiever she depicts in Howard Roark. Karen Andre is an excellent secretary; she can take any shorthand assignment Faulkner throws at her. She also becomes an expert at forging his signature. However, her productive capabilities are not on a par with later Rand heroines.

In *We the Living* the only person of actual achievement is Andrei. He is a hero whose bravery has been demonstrated in battle. At the Battle of Melitopol, he risks his life to convince the White Army soldiers in the trenches that the red flag should be their flag. His recognition of like quality in another is demonstrated when he first helps and then allows Captain Karsavin, one of the ablest of the White Army leaders, to commit suicide rather than risk capture. Though Kira and Leo have the raw materials for later achievement, neither of them is allowed to develop those natural resources. Kira has grand aspirations; she wants to be an engineer and build bridges and buildings. To that end she is a good student at the Technological Institute. Though the reader is convinced that she could be an able engineer, Kira is prevented from becoming one. She is expelled from the Institute because she is the daughter of a former factory owner. Her talents are buried in a deadening job as an excursion guide. Leo Kovalensky's only demonstrated talents are in the attraction of women. Though Kira believes in him and though he does begin study in the University, his promise is also stultified by the reverse discrimination practised against children of those who were once in power. Leo's only accomplishments are a bitter bravado and black marketeering.

In *We the Living* Rand had not yet fully developed her concept of the parasitical. The negative characters are more specifically opportunistic than parasitical. Of course, the opportunists are not productive and therefore as they do not contribute materially, they are in a very real sense feeding off the contributions of others. Not only are the Communists not productive, but their system does not promote productivity. What counts is not ability, but party membership or congeniality. Pavel Syerov trades upon his supposed friendship with Andrei Taganov, who is a real hero. He also benefits from the dangerous activities of speculators. They take the chances and he is paid off. Victor Dunaev has some real abilities, but he uses them to further his political aims, not to accomplish anything concrete.

It is not until *Anthem* that the Rand hero whose abilities are society-shaking in a positive sense is introduced. Equality 7–2521 is a creator and inventor in the tradition of Galileo, Edison, and Einstein. In a world where all technological advancement has been lost, he rediscovers electricity. Through hands-on experimentation, he is able to move beyond the shackles of his limited education. Not only does he invent, but he defies. When his society is not ready to accept what he offers, he escapes through uncharted forests to form a new colony of his own where he and others who wish to throw off the chains of collectivism can develop individually.

In *Anthem* there is really only one person of exceptional ability. There is a suggestion that International 4–8818 may be an artist with a real comic talent. And Liberty 5–3000 is brave and loyal. But the only one whose productive capabilities are fully displayed is Equality 7–2521. The villains in the story are not so much parasitical as inert and anti-progress. They do not want to benefit from Equality 7–2521's invention, nor do they want anyone else to.

The theme of the productive versus the parasitical is developed more fully in *The Fountainhead*. The term Rand uses to describe the parasitical in this work is "second-handers." One of the main plot lines of the novel traces the careers of the two architecture students the reader is introduced to in the first few chapters: Peter Keating and Howard Roark. Though Keating possesses a modicum of talent, rather than developing his gift, he guides his life by pursuing what other people think is important. He never learns his craft, and when important commissions are called for he must put his name on other people's work. When he achieves everything he thinks he should want, he does not understand the hollowness of it. He will never be satisfied because he has never gone after what he wants.

Howard Roark, on the other hand, knows exactly what he wants and is not the least bit interested in what other people think of it. In architectural terms, Roark's work is original. He does not follow an already established school or style. His designs proceed organically from the site and each building has an intrinsic integrity. As Roark explains to Austen Heller, "Your house is made by its own needs." The architecture produced by second-handers is derivative. John Erik Snyte's firm stocks one architect for each of a number of derivative styles: Classic, Gothic, Renaissance, and even Miscellaneous. Roark is hired because he fits the slot of "Modernistic."

What Roark respects is productivity. What he calls it is competence. He tells Gail Wynand that there is no substitute for it. Not all the love, personality, charity, good feeling in the world will hold up a poorly designed building.

Ability is the touchstone by which all of Roark's friends and Rand's characters are measured. The field does not matter. The social class does not matter. One of Roark's dearest friends is Mike, an electrician he meets on his first construction job. Mike, whose real name is Sean Xavier Donnigan, is passionate about his work and the people he respects are passionate about theirs; "He worshipped expertness. . . . " Once he is convinced about Roark's quality as an architect, he arranges to work on every one of Roark's commissions.

All of Roark's other friends, the ones who support him through the trial, are persons of exceptional accomplishment. Steve Mallory, who sculpts the statue of tribute to the human spirit, explains it. When Howard Roark wants to hear what he *thinks* and not who his family or friends are or about his childhood, he is overjoyed. He exclaims, "You want to know what I do and why I do it, you want to know what I think?" For Mallory, that means Roark really wants to know what counts about him. They become fast friends. Though Steve has been tried for attempted murder, what counts about him for Roark is his talent as a sculptor.

First-handers don't need others' approval. They know when what they have done is good. Peter Keating needs Ellsworth Toohey to tell him that he is a great architect. Second-handers need committees, and unions, and groups to reinforce themselves.

There is room in Rand's world for people who are not creative giants, but only if they are appreciative of those who create, who produce. In Rand's depiction of contemporary society this proper relationship has been overturned. Those who are unable to do have made the producers their slaves. In the characterization of employers as evil, the employee has forgotten that without the employer there would be no work.

The "second-handers" of *The Fountainhead* are the "moochers" and "looters" of *Atlas Shrugged*. While the "second-handers" are not productive and litter the cultural world with mediocre works, there is still room in the world of Howard Roark for genuine geniuses to function. In the world of *Atlas Shrugged* the "moochers" and "looters" not only hamper the producers' abilities to function, they pass laws and directives which confiscate both the means and the ends of their efforts.

One of John Galt's rationales for the "strike of the mind" is that if the weak have harnessed the strong to their service (as they claim the strong have exploited the weak in the past), then the strong should use the same means that the weak have used—a strike. When the productive withdraw their talents and abilities, the "looter" economy crumbles. When there is no host to feed on, a parasite cannot exist. This is the lesson that Rand teaches in *Atlas Shrugged*. In one of Francisco's speeches to Rearden he explains that Rearden is helping those who torment and hobble him because he still tries to produce even with all of the "looters'" restrictions. Francisco suggests that the only way to defeat looters is by not giving them anything to loot.

Certain motifs recur in Rand's fiction. The flamboyant or extravagant gesture is one. Bjorn Faulkner gives Karen Andre a dress of platinum mesh; "Guts" Regan sends her one pound of orchids; Hank Rearden buys Dagny an exorbitantly priced pear-shaped ruby to wear for his eyes alone; Dominique purchases a priceless sculpture of Helios from a museum and then destroys it because she considers it too beautiful for a world of second-handers. For Rand's characters, these gestures indicate freedom from monetary and mundane restraints.

Music also plays an important role in Rand's works. It symbolizes the creative and inspirational capacities of humanity. *We the Living* and *Atlas Shrugged* have the strongest musical components. For Kira, "The Song of Broken Glass," a tune from an operetta, encapsulates a sense of the gaiety and joy possible in life. Its promising notes echo in her brain as she dies. Richard Halley's unpublished Fifth Concerto initiates Dagny's search for the great minds that have vanished. Its triumphant strains reverberate in her head through much of the book. As Ayn Rand's body lay in state, light operetta music played as the crowds paid her their last respects.

Trials act as significant plot junctures in the majority of Rand's works of fiction. The most important trial in terms of plot structure is Howard Roark's arraignment for blowing up the Cortlandt Housing Project. His acquittal is evidence that justice can prevail and that the individualist does not have to be destroyed. Hank Rearden's trial for defying an unfair government edict also results in his winning. In Rearden's case, he contests the court's jurisdiction over him. In both of these trials, the accused act as their own defense attorneys and in both their summation speeches are important statements of Rand's philosophy of personal rights. Since the juries agree with the accused in each case, one could infer that Rand has faith that an average dozen citizens will respond to reason and appreciate greatness. *Night of January 16th* is a courtroom drama. The trial is the plot of this play. There are also trials in *Anthem* and *We the Living*. But whereas the trials in *The Fountainhead* and *Atlas Shrugged* demonstrate the value of the jury system, the trials in the former works are travesties of justice. When Equality 7–2521 will not tell where he has been, he is sent to the Palace of Corrective Detention without a trial. There, on the instruction of two Judges, he is lashed repeatedly. Later, his actions and invention are condemned by the ignorance of The World Council of Scholars. When Kira and Leo go to the People's Court to protest the fact that one of their rooms is taken from them, they are judged not on the merits of their case, but upon their ancestry.

Cities, especially those with a skyscraper skyline, are the preferred setting for Rand's stories. Skyscrapers serve as a positive symbol. They represent the potential for human conquest over nature. Rand is not ecology-minded. She is enamored of technology and the urban landscape. Kira's chosen profession is engineering. She keeps a picture of an American skyscraper over her bed. Howard Roark's most important commission is the Wynand Building, which will tower over Hell's Kitchen in New York. When Dagny walks on the streets of New York, she is filled with reverence by the sight of the skyline. Rand is the antithesis of a primitivist. Her characters are not refreshed by interaction with nature. For them, nature is there to be harnessed.

The following summaries provide individual overviews of each of Rand's four novels, her one published play, and her one published short story. *We the Living*, *Night of January 16th*, and *Anthem* have been published in revised versions. My discussion derives from the latest editions.

We the Living (1936)

Begun only four years after she arrived in this country, We the Living is, among other things, the fulfillment of a promise Rand made to a guest at the farewell party her family gave for her before she left for America. A man asked her to communicate to Americans that life in Russia was stultifying and that Soviet society was moribund.

We the Living explicates convincingly the detrimental effects of the Soviet government. The novel is remarkable for a number of reasons, not the least of which is the author's impressive ability to communicate complex and subtle ideological arguments in a newly learned language. Rand explains in the foreword to the current edition that she did line editing in 1958 to remove some of the awkward construction in the 1936 edition; she also reworded for purposes of clarity. She claims that the revision was minimal. Some readers of both editions have questioned her definition of "minimal." Nonetheless, like Joseph Conrad and Vladimir Nabokov, two other literary giants for whom English was not a native language, she displays an astonishing virtuosity in what was not her native tongue.

Rand comments in the foreword that We the Living is as close to an autobiographical work as she would ever write, but that the extent of its resemblance to her life is that she and the heroine hold similar convictions. Though the details of their lives may differ, it is easy to infer from Kira's story why Rand hated the Marxist system.

The plot of We the Living concerns a young woman's struggle to fulfill her capabilities under the frustrating strictures of a Communist regime. Not only is Kira not permitted to complete her engineering studies so she can build the bridges and skyscrapers she has dreamed of constructing, but she is not permitted to leave Russia so that she might follow her dream in another part of the world. Lest any reader misinterpret Rand's message about the effects of the Communist revolution, through her spokesperson, Kira, Rand makes it clear that the revolution did not fail because it was betrayed (a common argument from those who would indict the particular Soviet system while still embracing the fundamental tenets of communism). Rand explicitly indicts the ideology that fueled the revolution—the supremacy of the collective over the individual. Through Kira's and other characters' stories Rand illustrates why such an ideology is detrimental to humanity's capacities for productivity and fulfillment. It glorifies mediocrity, or worse, while stifling the good and the best.

Andrei Taganov is one of the most tragic characters in the book. He is a hero of the revolution, one who sincerely attempts to bring his sisters and brothers up to a humane level of existence. Reacting in good faith to the deprivations he had suffered as a child, he sees communism as a system for the alleviation of the horrors of Czarist Russia. It is only after he experiences the system in action that he begins to realize the magnitude of his miscalculation.

We the Living chronicles the experiences of Kira Argounova, young, bright, and full of enthusiasm for life. The plot begins when her family returns to Petrograd to begin life anew after the revolution. The year is 1922. The family factories have been nationalized and the Argounov home appropriated for living quarters for a number of families. After a life of luxury, the family must learn to cope with the long lines, shortages, and discrimination against the bourgeoisie that characterize the new regime. Kira becomes a student at the Technological Institute where she meets Andrei Taganov, the hero of Melitopol and other battles of the revolution. Though they are worlds apart ideologically and socially, they are attracted to each other and develop a mutual respect. Eventually, Andrei falls in love with Kira. Though she cares deeply for him, she never returns his love in kind.

Kira, in a pattern duplicated by later Rand heroines, falls in love instantaneously with Leo Kovalensky, whom she meets accidently on a street in Petrograd. Without knowing anything about him, she is willing to trust her safety to him. Kira and Leo try to escape Russia, but when that fails, they move in together. Though they struggle valiantly to keep their relationship free from pain and drudgery, Leo cannot bring himself to compromise with the system and therefore loses his job. When Leo develops tuberculosis, Kira becomes Andrei's mistress in order to have access to food and money so she can save Leo's life. The situation is ultimately intolerable and Leo cynically adopts a life of debauchery. Andrei commits suicide and Kira is killed trying to cross the border.

In the interim, the reader is shown many of the abuses of a totalitarian state and a revolution gone sour as its system is worked to the benefit of "speculators" and plunderers. Rand describes a drab, dull, deadening society. When party membership rather than ability is the prerequisite for position, progress is undermined and productivity slowed. When individual interests are sacrificed to that vague misnomer "the good of the group," those who would create and contribute color to a society cannot function.

Though it is set specifically in Soviet Russia from 1922 to 1925, and though it details much of what life was like in those post-revolutionary times, *We the Living* is about more than that particular time and place. It is a novel about the individual against the collective, an iconoclastic work for the 1930s when the bulk of belles-lettres in America was, if not decidedly leftist, then certainly left-leaning. The worker and the common man and woman became the central figures of much early twentieth-century fiction. For Rand the common and mediocre were not fit subjects for idealization. Though she expresses faith in the good sense of the average American (her juries usually react rationally), her central characters are exceptional people. Though she includes characters in her works who are victims, her protagonists are those who defy the system, who will not give in.

While it does not have the power of *The Fountainhead* nor the majestic sweep of *Atlas Shrugged*, *We the Living* is still a compelling story about interesting characters. Its depiction of the day-by-day spirit-destroying activities of life in Russia places it in a group with *One Day in the Life of Ivan Denisovich*, *Doctor Zhivago*, and other indictments from within and without the pale.

Night of January 16th (1936)

Rand's first professional writing was in the presentational rather than the representational mode. When she was still inexperienced with the language, writing scenarios which others could then flesh out into scripts was a natural starting place. While she was employed by Cecil B. De Mille, she wrote screen scenarios, but as she became more facile in the language, she began to write movie scripts. Her first major sale was the screenplay for an original movie. A good part of her early career was spent either in direct or indirect contact with the movie industry. Her first public success, however, was in the theatre.

Called *Penthouse Legend* by its author, produced in Hollywood under the title *Woman on Trial*, Rand's first play opened on Broadway in 1935 with the current title, *Night of January 16th*, and had a successful half-year run.

Night of January 16th is significant for dramatic ingenuity and the-matic content. It is because of the latter area that Rand had to contin-ually battle her producer. He wanted to excise the "value" preaching which Rand saw as the determining factor in the jury's ability to judge the heroine's guilt or innocence.

The plot is structured around a trial. All the action takes place in the courtroom. The protagonist, Karen Andre, is accused of murdering Bjorn Faulkner, who was her boss and her lover. There are conflicting stories about whether Faulkner jumped or was pushed from her penthouse ledge.

Bjorn Faulkner had been a free-wheeling, world-class entrepreneur whose financial kingdom was in desperate straits at the time of his death. Two versions of the state of his psyche are presented in court: The pros-ecution pictures him as a man, reformed by the love of a good woman, who was being blackmailed by his ex-mistress and her gangster lover; the defense contends that Faulkner never changed, that he used himself as collateral so that John Graham Whitfield would extend a ten million dollar loan; his marriage to Nancy Whitfield was a sham.

At the end of Act II, in a dramatic reversal, "Guts" Regan, the gangster and alleged lover of Karen Andre, shows up to announce that Bjorn Faulkner is really dead. He explains that he, Karen, and Bjorn had planned a fake suicide so that Bjorn and Karen could disappear with Whitfield's money. The body the police found was that of an already dead gangster in Bjorn's clothes. Regan contends and Faulkner's book-keeper verifies the fact that Whitfield found out about the money being transferred to a bank in Brazil. Regan accuses Whitfield of murdering Faulkner. The jury is left to decide whether a respected banker and his socialite daughter or a secretary-mistress and a gangster in the protection rackets are telling the truth.

Rand called this a "sense of life" play. The characters' actions are meant to be symbolic. Rand got the idea for her plot from the story of the sui-cide of Ivar Kreuger, a Swede who came to this country with a hundred dollars and built an international financial empire so vast that he loaned money to nations and controlled half the match industry of the world. After he killed himself, it was discovered that this man, who was imaged in the public mind as "legendary" and a "genius," had falsified records and that his match kingdom was bankrupt. Whether Kreuger was the victim of bad economic winds or a master criminal was the subject of public debate. Like Icarus, he flew too high and was burned. Rand con-tends that the press excoriated him, not for his fall, but for his flight. The *New York Times* coverage, however, was generally sympathetic and portrayed Kreuger as a man who was caught in a situation beyond his control, a man whose largesse benefited many countries.

Anthem (1938)

If any of Rand's works becomes a staple on high school reading lists, it will be this book. Because of its brevity and parable-like quality, it, like Steinbeck's *The Pearl* or *Of Mice and Men*, communicates to in-dividuals of greatly varying levels of experience and sophistication. One can read it, when young, and assimilate its essential message; the more one lives and works in a world of committees and councils, the more one's recognition is activated by the implications of Rand's portrayal of the possible results when collectivist ideology is taken to its logical ex-tension.

Anthem, like Walter Van Tilburg Clark's "The Portable Phono-graph," or Stephan Vincent Benet's "By the Waters of Babylon," depicts a world after some great war or nuclear holocaust has destroyed all tech-nological apparatus. In *Anthem* society has returned to an era of illu-mination by candlelight. Whereas the world has moved backwards in terms of the benefits of science and technology, the structuring philosophy for the society is the "one world" and "good of the group" ideology which is preached as the goal of so many altruistic political movements of our age. Rand shows us just what it would be like to live for the good of our society rather than ourselves. The picture is not pleasant.

Unlike her other works, in which Rand acts as the omniscient narrator, *Anthem* is narrated by its hero; Equality 7–2521 is twenty-one years old and because he is taller and brighter than most of his brothers, he is viewed suspiciously by the elders of his society. Much of the pleasure of the story derives from the readers' uses of their imaginations as they fill in the gaps in the hero's knowledge of the "unmentionable times" before the ascendence of the collectivist society. Equality 7–2521 attempts to fight the "evil" in himself which pushes him to learn more and do more than others, but cannot. He commits the "sin of preference" and desires to be sent to the Home of the Scholars, for he has a great thirst for knowledge; The Council of Vocations, however, punishes him and sentences him at the age of fifteen to the job of street sweeper for life.

In the course of his drudgery, Equality 7–2521 discovers the remains of an ancient subway and there, using stolen materials, he begins conducting scientific experiments. Though he knows that what he is doing is unlawful in his society, the joy of learning fills his heart and he keeps his activity a secret. Committing another "sin of preference," he falls in love with Liberty 5–3000 whom he sees in the fields. She returns his love, and when he must escape the city, she follows him into the Uncharted Forest.

The sin that drives Equality 7–2521 from the society of his brothers is the discovery of electricity, which he would share with the Council of Scholars, but which they reject because it was not a group creation and because it would threaten the Department of Candles. Like many creators before him, Equality 7–2521 is perceived as a threat to the established order.

Once free of their restrictive society, Equality 7–2521 and Liberty 5–3000 rediscover the knowledge of the "unmentionable time"; they discover the self and free will. Having discovered the "I," they adopt the names Prometheus and Gaea and set about to build a fortress from which they will fight to reclaim the freedom that humanity had lost by its own lack of foresight.

Anthem was published in England in 1938, but not in this country until 1946 when Pamphleteers, which did not generally publish fiction, brought it out in an abridged paperback edition; later Caxton Press issued it in hardback. The New American Library paperback edition has gone through numerous printings. There is even a comic-book version that was published in 1953.

The Fountainhead (1943)

Although followers of Ayn Rand's philosophy accept *Atlas Shrugged* as the fullest explication of Objectivism, from a strictly literary perspective *The Fountainhead* is a better novel. Both extoll the same individualistic virtues, but *The Fountainhead* does so in a more concise and unified manner.

Rand chose the world of contemporary architecture as the setting for her exploration of the difference between beings whose souls are self-actualized and those second-handers whose values are all derived not from any inner urgings, but from what others find valuable. What Rand puts forth in *The Fountainhead* is a rationale for "selfishness" or egoism as a moral good. Architecture is an apt backdrop for Rand's explication because it is simultaneously an art, a science, and a business, and thus representative of all professions.

Howard Roark, *The Fountainhead*'s protagonist and hero, is an architect. A man of unswerving integrity and exceptional ability, he is guided by no values but his own. The plot follows his career from the day he is expelled from the Architecture School of Stanton Institute of Technology through his difficulties in establishing himself as a working architect to his professional and personal victory and vindication. He diverges from his code on rare occasions, and then only in full knowledge of what he is doing.

Juxtaposed against Roark are three other men: Peter Keating, Ellsworth Toohey, and Gail Wynand. Each represents a variation of spiritual collectivism. Gail Wynand, the most tragic figure in *The Fountainhead*, is a cynic who has qualities of greatness, but his disillusionment with his fellow creatures has caused him to seek control over others. Too late, he learns that those he thinks he controls, control him instead. Ellsworth Toohey is as vicious a villain as contemporary literature presents. His goal is power and he is fully cognizant of the effects of the destructive means he employs toward his ends. By extolling ineptness and mediocrity, Toohey undermines ability and quality; the talentless thereby remain under his influence and the forces that would oppose him are reduced. Peter Keating rises to the top of his profession by manipulating people rather than creating sound architectural designs. Keating is a man whose entire life is ruled by others to his own detriment. The outer trappings of success bring him little lasting satisfaction and eventually he loses even those.

Dominique Francon, Rand's heroine, is an interesting case study in perverseness. She is so convinced of the triumph of evil that she submits herself to every possible degradation lest she chance to hope. She is physically and psychologically masochistic: she is raped by Roark; she marries two men she despises. Dominique's personality, Rand claims, is a representation of herself when she is in a bad mood. Dominique is beautiful and talented. She is desired in different ways by all the main characters, good or evil. When she finally becomes convinced of the error of her ways, she commits herself to becoming Mrs. Howard Roark and sharing his life and happiness.

The novel's climactic scene is a trial at which Howard Roark stands accused of blowing up a housing project that he surreptitiously designed. Peter Keating took credit for the design, but in his contract with Roark promised that the plans would not be altered in any way. Roark blows up the project when his contract is not honored and his plans are bastardized beyond recognition. He is exonerated after a thematic speech in which he spells out the significance of the individual creator who, though often damned rather than blessed for his contributions to human progress and happiness, is at the crux of every major human advance. Roark explains that creativity is an individual thing—that the creator works for the joy of the creation, the work being an end in itself. The group may then benefit, but that is a by-product rather than the goal of the creator. He reminds the jury that this country was created on the principle that the pursuit of happiness is an inalienable right and that that happiness is the happiness of the individual. He spells out the credo he lives by, "I recognize no obligations toward men except one: to respect their freedom and to take no part in a slave society."

Rand's book ends with the triumph of integrity and individualism. She believes that against good, evil is impotent. It is only when the good compromises that it loses its ability to withstand evil. *The Fountainhead* can be read as a modern version of a medieval morality play. Each of its characters represents a variation on the continuum between good and evil. In an age where realism and naturalism reign in character depiction, this seems an anachronism. In twentieth-century fiction the larger-than-life hero and the unregenerate villain are rare. Though architecture is not the real subject of *The Fountainhead*, the book also reads like a debate among schools of architectural design. Rand did extensive research into the subject and then worked in the office of Eli Jacques Kahn, a famous New York architect. Her knowledge of architecture is evident throughout the book. Many readers have presumed that the character of Roark was based on Frank Lloyd Wright; however, Rand contends that the only similarity is that both were innovators fighting for modernism as opposed to traditionalism in architecture. Rand is not for parasitism or derivativeness of any kind, so it follows that her hero would design buildings unlike any that had ever been built before.

In *The Fountainhead* Rand describes the growth of Roark's career by comparing it to a stream that develops below the ground, quietly and unobserved, but then bursts forth, bubbling to the surface until it builds into a full torrent. Rand later commented that she did not·know that she was also describing the story of her book's popularity. Originally declined by some publishers because they did not think the book would be "commercial," *The Fountainhead* has continued to sell well since its original publication.

Atlas Shrugged (1957)

Atlas Shrugged has been described by more than one critic as "The Bible" of Objectivism. Rand was fond of quoting it and on more than one occasion told a questioner that if they wanted to know about Rand's philosophy, they need only read *Atlas Shrugged*. The novel has had great appeal, however, to millions who have never heard of Objectivism.

Atlas Shrugged can satisfy any number of tastes. It has been described as a work of science fiction, a mystery story, a female fantasy novel, and a theodicy of capitalism. Regardless of how one approaches it, there is story enough to please all but the most zealous critic. There are adventure, excitement, mystery, romance, surprises, and material for mental mastication. It also has the most heroic female protagonist in American fiction: Dagny Taggart.

Dagny runs Taggart Transcontinental Railroad though her brother, James, is its titular president. He is a weak, indecisive man, given to petty cruelties. In order to keep the railroad functioning properly, she must work around and override him. Her task is complicated by networks of bureaus, councils, and committees and their by-products: lack of responsibility, ineptness, frustration. The capable seem to be "dropping out." Pride in craftsmanship and earning one's way have become practically nonexistent. At this point the reader thinks the setting must be here and now and that one is reading a realistic story. It is because of this aspect of the novel that Rand has been called prophetic. She is particularly good at describing the failings of collectivist institutions, especially big government.

As things keep breaking down, Dagny sets about to rebuild one of Taggart's old lines, and it is during that task that she contacts Hank Rearden, a steel tycoon and the inventor of a new kind of metal that is better than steel. They become lovers and battle to keep the economy running although they must fight even those who claim to be on their side. Ironically, they are fighting their natural allies, other able individualists, who have gone on a "strike of the mind."

Three questions plague Dagny: who is the inventor of an abandoned motor she finds in the ruins of an old factory? where are all the capable people going? and who is John Galt? The latter is a slang expression that is in general use, conveying a sense of despair. Much of the plot concerns Dagny's attempt to find the answers to those questions.

Her search leads her to discover a utopian community in the mountains of Colorado where the "drop-outs" have set up their own free-enterprise system. Alternately called Mulligan's Valley or Galt's Gulch, this society serves as a refuge from the "looters," "scabs," and "moochers," who live off the productivity of others while contributing nothing to the society. Born as a reaction against the collectivist maxim, "From each according to his ability; to each according to his need," this community's motto is "I swear by my life and my love of it that I will never live for the sake of another man nor ask another man to live for mine."

But Dagny does not stay in the paradisiacal valley; she is not yet ready to leave the world to the "looters." Inspired by the vision of Hank Rearden and those like him who still have the courage to fight the "moochers," Dagny resolves to try till the end. She returns to a world in shambles. Outbreaks of violence, general despair, a bankrupt economy, and a nation of inept leaders face world crisis.

A national broadcast by Mr. Thompson, the head of state, is announced. As the whole country waits for some reassuring words, the airwaves are commandeered by the "men of the mind," and in a dissertation-length speech, John Galt spells out the tenets of a rational philosophy: the necessity of choice, the virtue of reason, the importance of independence, the responsibility of judgment. He also explains the causes of the global crisis: mysticism, the concept of Original Sin, altruism, and what he calls the "cult of zero-worship." He exhorts those remaining to withdraw, to vanish, never to let their strength be used by the weak.

After a melodramatic confrontation during which the desperate "looters" torture Galt in an attempt to get him to take over and restore the economy, the parasites are finally vanquished. The motor of the world stops, represented by the blackout of the lights of New York City. The strike has succeeded. The productive and creative can return to rebuild.

Atlas Shrugged is a very long and complex novel and no summary can do justice to its plot and subplots. Francisco d'Anconia and Ragnar Danneskjöld, two of its most fascinating heroic characters, have not been mentioned. The novel also boasts a listing of villainous characters that equals Pope's *Dunciad* for vituperative description and enumeration. Besides the major characters, there are a variety of secondary characters who represent both positive and negative aspects of numerous professions and avocations. Rand's portrait of a crumbling society is an encompassing one.

By the time *Atlas Shrugged* was published, Rand was a well-known author and a large readership was anxiously awaiting its appearance. It had been fourteen years since the publication of *The Fountainhead*. Although it did not receive a welcoming reception by most critics, it has been in print both in hardback and paperback since its original publication.

"The Simplest Thing in the World"

Though it was written in 1940, this short story was not published until twenty-seven years later in *The Objectivist*,and then in *The Romantic Manifesto* in 1969. It is the only published short story by Rand.

The title is ironic; Henry Dorn, the protagonist, is trying to convince himself that the simplest thing in the world would be to write formula fiction. However, for a man of his creative abilities, it is anything but simple to force his mind into mundane patterns.

Most of the story takes place in his mind as he battles his natural inclinations and tries to force himself to write for the commercial market. As Rand explained in the headnote, "The story illustrates the nature of the creative process—the way in which an artist's sense of life directs the integrating functions of his subconscious and controls his creative imagination."

CHAPTER 3

A Compendium of Characters

Character may be the most significant element in Ayn Rand's fiction. To her, literary personages are of such importance that she found the image of one, Enjolras, the brave, passionate defender of right and liberty in Victor Hugo's *Les Miserables*, sufficient to sustain her when she faced the possibility of death as a young girl in revolutionary Russia. Part of her credo of literature is that the writer of fiction should populate her stories with individuals who inspire us, ideal characters, people we would want to meet, rather than characters like the people next door. Over and over again, in her writing career, she resisted the direction of movie studio editors or publishing house executives who enjoined her to write about "realistic people," people she might meet on the street. What has been depicted by critics as her "stylized vice-and-virtue character(s)" is not a fault, but results from a conscious literary decision.

The purpose of this chapter, then, is to provide an index to those virtuous and villainous fictional characters who symbolize the ideal and the evil in humanity. Most of Rand's characters fall neatly into one or the other of those categories, though there are a few crossover or neutral characters. For the sake of organization, I have classified Rand's significant fictional characters into six categories: (1) the heroic protagonists; (2) other primary heroic personages; (3) characters of virtue but lesser import; (4) the archvillainous antagonists; (5) secondary unworthy or villainous characters; (6) neutral or metamorphosing characters. The characters will be organized according to the literary work in which they appear. Within each work, the characters will be arranged alphabetically.

THE HEROIC PROTAGONISTS

Rand's protagonists share many traits. They are all Romantic rebels against restrictive and mundane societies. In their rebellion, they act alone and on principle. Though, in some cases, they may be joined by the like-minded, that factor is never crucial to their revolt. They are all intellectually gifted and have unusual talents. The modern literary term for the main character is "protagonist," which means the chief striver, rather than hero. The protagonist is the character whose struggle or story is the main focus of the plot. This term is appropriate in modern fiction because many of the main characters in contemporary literature are anything but heroic. In Rand's case, however, the traditional terminology would be applicable. All her protagonists are also heroes.

We the Living

Kira Alexandrovna Argounova   Kira is the closest to an autobiographical character that Rand creates. Though Rand claims that Kira is autobiographical only in that she and Kira share beliefs, there are also some details of their lives that are parallel. Both are young students at the time of the Russian revolution. Both are daughters of prosperous businessmen whose businesses were nationalized by the Communist government. Kira is described as slender and proud, with a defiant posture; pictures of Ayn Rand show a similar woman. As a young girl Kira is inspired by the character of a Viking in a story; Ayn Rand's literary hero was Cyrus, a brave, arrogant, and daring British officer in a children's story. Unwilling to adjust to the Communist regime, Ayn Rand received a passport to leave Russia in 1925; Kira Argounova, whose passport application is refused, is killed trying to cross the Latvian border. Kira is young, eighteen when the novel begins, gray-eyed, with brown hair, and with a determination not to let the collectivist system wear her down. She wants to be an engineer and build steel structures; the only career, other than writing, that Rand considered was engineering. Kira rejects religion and treacly fairytales, and once she has encountered the man she loves, Leo Kovalensky, she is willing to do anything to secure his health and well-being. Unmindful of her material surroundings, she wants only to be allowed to fulfill the best that is in her.

Night of January 16th

Karen Andre   A proud, defiant animal underlies the cool, calm, detached persona that Karen Andre projects on the witness stand. Slender and elegant, Karen wears her simple, tailored clothes with the authority of timeless fashion. The prosecution witnesses characterize her as shameless and pagan, a primitive seductress who would rather kill the man she loves than allow him to be happy with another woman. The defense portrays her as a capable, loyal, passionately-in-love woman who is willing to do anything, including forgery and fraud, to aid her lover, Bjorn Faulkner. Karen and Bjorn are lovers and business associates from the first day he hires her as his secretary. Karen is twenty-eight at the time of the trial. Though her fate is decided at each performance by a jury made up of twelve members of the audience, Rand, obviously, considers her "NOT GUILTY."

Anthem

Equality 7–2521   Six feet tall, twenty-one years old, and equipped with a quick and inquisitive mind in a futuristic society which values only sameness, Equality 7–2521 must forge a difficult path to identity. Defying the edicts of his brothers, he experiments with electricity to become the literal and figurative bringer of light, like Prometheus, whose name he eventually takes. The woman he loves, Liberty 5–3000, thinks of him as "The Unconquered" and together they escape their collectivist society to build a fort of individualism from which he and his chosen friends can begin their battle for freedom, rights and honor.

The Fountainhead

Howard Roark   When the novel begins, Howard is a young architecture student. He is encountered naked and laughing, an innocent Adam, poised on a cliff. Roark's looks have comic-strip color and clarity: orange hair and gray eyes, a contemptuous mouth, a sure and self-sufficient attitude. He cares nothing about what other people think of him. The quality he demands in his friends is a "self-sufficient ego." He does not see a love relationship as an amalgamation of beings. He believes that in order to say "I love you," one must first be able to be an "I." Roark is a brilliant architect, unwilling to compromise the integrity of his creations for the sake of monetary gains. The only compromises Roark makes are for either Dominique, the woman he loves, or Gail Wynand, his friend. In these cases, he is true to himself, for they are people he values. He is, in Peter Keating's words, "the most egotistical and the kindest man." Consistent to the end, he is able to convince a jury of the validity of his position after he blows up a housing project for the poor. His plan for the project was altered, contrary to his contract. After his exoneration, Gail Wynand contracts with him to build the tallest skyscraper in New York City, the Wynand Building, even though Wynand has lost his wife, Dominique, to Roark and his newspaper, the *Banner,* in fighting Roark's cause. The building is to be a tribute to Roark's spirit.

Atlas Shrugged

Dagny Taggart   Dagny Taggart is probably the most admirable and successful heroine in American fiction. Not only is her worth acclaimed by her allies, but even her enemies acknowledge her extraordinary abilities. As Vice-President in Charge of Operation, she runs Taggart Transcontinental, the largest railroad in the country, though her brother James is the titular head. In her early thirties, young-looking, slender, with shapely legs and medium-length brown hair, she does not look the part of a railroad tycoon. Her authority derives from her ability. Her first lover is Francisco d'Anconia, but his inexplicable transition into a playboy leaves her hurt and dismayed. She accepts the challenge of rebuilding the Rio Norte Line (which she renames The John Galt Line) and in the process develops a relationship with Hank Rearden, who helps fund the line. Though he is married, she becomes his mistress. Together they try to keep the national economy from falling apart. Dagny fights longer than any of the people of accomplishment against giving the world over to the "moochers and looters." Even after she meets and falls in love with John Galt and understands the nature of his strike, she will not give up her railroad. At the conclusion of the novel Dagny and John Galt, along with the other "people of the mind," are ready to return and rebuild.

"The Simplest Thing in the World"

Henry Dorn   Henry Dorn is the author of a book called *Triumph* which was anything but what its name suggests. The critics had either not liked or misunderstood it. As his wife Kitty plays solitaire, Dorn sits at his desk trying to write a simple story, one the public would like. But each story he concocts in his mind takes his imagination on flights of philosophical fancy and he knows that what may be the simplest thing in the world for people without integrity is impossible for him.

OTHER PRIMARY HEROIC PERSONAGES

The following characters are often of equal stature with the protagonist in that they either embody equivalent values or are adjuncts in the quest to maintain or discover the good.

We the Living

Leo Kovalensky   Though he is not an ideal male, Leo Kovalensky is the prototype for later Rand heroes. Like other Rand protagonists, he has haughty eyes and a contemptuous smile, and looks as if he were born to carry a whip. Described as handsome enough to model for a bust of Apollo, straight, tall, and proud even in his penurious state, Leo succumbs to cynicism and becomes a gigolo, hell-bent for destruction. Leo serves as an example of how the injustices of collectivism destroy the fine and the able. Though Kira adores Leo as the embodiment of her highest values, he turns out to be unworthy of her sacrifices in his behalf.

Andrei Taganov   One of Rand's most sympathetic misguided but worthy characters, Andrei is a Communist, a fearless soldier, an heroic revolutionary. Battle-scarred, with the look of a tamed tiger, Andrei has had a difficult childhood which leads him naturally into revolution against a system which has oppressed him and his family. Ascetic, and passionately devoted to bringing the masses up to his level, he only learns the full extent of the party's corruption in the course of his G.P.U. work. Though he has been betrayed by Kira, he understands her reasons and continues to help her. His integrity will not allow him to remain silent about the betrayal of the revolution, and he comes to realize that even its ideals were not valid.

Night of January 16th

Bjorn Faulkner   Although he never appears in the play, Bjorn Faulkner's character is the focus of the plot. He is strong and audacious. Other men's rules do not hamper him. He is willing to swindle, forge, and even sell himself as security for his financial empire. A man who takes what he wants, he also gives generously. He is a man of flamboyant gestures; he gives Karen a fine platinum mesh gown, which when heated and slipped on her, has a more erotic effect than nudity. The audience is asked to judge if such a man could change his ways and settle down with a socialite wife or if, to the end, he would remain a man of such self-esteem, of such overweening spirit, that he would not be conquered except by death. Rand based his character on Ivar Kreuger, the Swedish "Match King" who committed suicide when his empire collapsed in 1932.

Larry "Guts" Regan   Tall and slender, with light eyes and an assured manner, "Guts" Regan is a notorious outlaw whose main enterprise is running a protection racket. Because of his love for Karen, which is the one good and true thing that ever happened to him, "Guts" is willing to participate in the fake suicide of Bjorn Faulkner. He even procures the body of a murdered gunman to substitute for Faulkner's body. He is accused by the district attorney of helping Karen to murder Bjorn, though he claims that Whitfield is the real culprit and that the latter paid him $5,000 to keep quiet about discovering Whitfield's car near the field Faulkner was to use for his getaway.

Anthem

Liberty 5–3000   Seventeen, straight, and "thin as a blade of iron," Liberty 5–3000 is thought of by Equality 7–2521 as "The Golden One." Her eyes are dark and project a hard, glowing, and fearless quality. She knows no guilt. She is brave and single-minded, for she goes alone into the Uncharted Forest to follow Equality 7–2521. She takes the name of Gaea, for she will give birth to a new breed of godlike humans.

The Fountainhead

Dominique Francon   Dominique is a beautiful woman, with a body so exquisite that she models for a statue of tribute to the indomitable human spirit. Dominique's fragile appearance, pale gold hair, and gray eyes belie a capable, cynical, and disarmingly blunt manner. Proceeding from the conviction that good has no chance in this world, a premise that is the opposite of Rand's belief, Dominique chooses not to care about anything in order not to let anything or anyone have power over her. Rand has characterized Dominique as "myself in a bad mood." Masochistic in the extreme, Dominique marries men she despises in order to prove to herself that she does not care. She has a strong perverse streak—she tries to destroy Roark, the man she loves, even though she hopes she will not be able to do so. Whenever she does something particularly hurtful to him, she goes to him and sleeps with him. Her marriage to Peter Keating is ended by Gail Wynand, who buys Dominique from Peter for $250,000 and the Stoneridge commission. Though Dominique begins the marriage to Wynand as an expression of self-contempt, she learns to care for him. Only when Gail Wynand, in order to save the *Banner*, gives up his battle to protect Roark does Dominique, openly and in a scandalous manner, give Wynand reason to divorce her. By the end of the novel, Dominique has learned to accept happiness and live openly and unafraid as Mrs. Howard Roark.

Gail Wynand   Wynand is one of Rand's most tragic characters. As a young boy he pulls himself out of the miserable environment of Hell's Kitchen in search of beauty and integrity. His quest brings disillusionment and cynicism, and in his bitterness he looks for people of quality and integrity only in order to break them. He surrenders himself to the vulgar and the mediocre, turning his newspaper, the *Banner*, into a cheap scandal sheet, full of crime and sentiment. He is described by Austen

Heller as "an exquisite bastard." Paying with his honor for unlimited power leaves him with nothing more to conquer; bored and in a state of misanthropy, he is ready to play Russian roulette. Dominique's statue renews his interest in life. Unfortunately, Wynand meets Dominique and Howard Roark too late. Having given himself over to second-handers, he cannot use his newspaper effectively when he decides to battle for positive values. Though he fights valiantly to save Roark, in the end he capitulates and then cannot forgive himself. He divorces Dominique, closes down the *Banner*, but does give Roark the Wynand Building commission which includes a proviso that he and Howard are never to meet again.

Atlas Shrugged

Francisco d'Anconia   Born to aristocracy and wealth, Francisco d'Anconia begins in his youth to develop his considerable natural abilities. By tradition every d'Anconia, since the first ancestor fled the Inquisition, must earn the right to the name and leave the family fortune larger than when he received it. A man with great *joie de vivre*, he looks the part of nobility. Tall, slender, dark-haired and blue-eyed, he carries himself with style, as if a cape were unfurling behind him. While still in college, he works his way from furnace boy to factory owner, and by the age of twenty-three he is the copper king of the world. Then, inexplicably, he changes. At thirty-six he has the reputation of a dissipated playboy. Francisco is Dagny's first love and later he becomes Hank Rearden's friend. His is the job of reeducating Rearden; to that end he delivers several of the most important theoretical speeches in the novel: the oration that contains the title imagery and the renunciation of the money-is-the-root-of-all-evil concept. He tries to convince both Hank and Dagny to stop placing their abilities at the service of second-raters. Francisco pays the highest price for his ideals: he loses Dagny first to Rearden and then to John Galt; he destroys the d'Anconia mines. Nevertheless, his strength of character and devotion to his ideals make him capable of absorbing all the losses and still reaping joy out of his existence.

Ragnar Danneskjöld   One of the triumvirate that sets out to stop the motor of the world, Ragnar, scion of European aristocracy, first meets his lifelong friends, Francisco d'Anconia and John Galt, when he is a freshman at Patrick Henry University. Ragnar is an incredibly beautiful man with hair of gold and the audacity of a buccaneer. A gentle and delicate intellectual, he had originally chosen philosophy as his field, but he becomes an international pirate, sinking ships laden with foreign aid or important raw materials. He blows up Orren Boyle's furnaces to prevent Boyle from manufacturing the ill-gotten formula for Rearden Metal. One of his goals is to destroy the myth of Robin Hood. Rather than steal from the rich and give to the poor, he steals from the undeserving and gives to the deserving. Danneskjöld's part in the novel is not as large as d'Anconia's, Rearden's or Galt's, but as an ideal he completes the picture of how men of ability and integrity must respond to a world of moochers and looters. He is married to Kay Ludlow, the actress, and their marriage is an illustration of a relationship of equals.

John Galt   The ideal hero or code hero of *Atlas Shrugged*, John Galt is the man who stops the motor of the world when he leads the "men of the mind" on strike against all the leeches and parasites they have been sustaining throughout history. It is John who as a young engineer at Twentieth Century Motors revolts against the collectivist credo and says, "I will put an end to this, once and for all." Self-made and self-educated, John Galt leaves his home somewhere in Ohio and as a student is the most promising young physicist ever to matriculate at Patrick Henry University. He calls his friends, Francisco and Ragnar, to join him and become "flame-spotters," who find flares of genius and convince other productive individuals to join them in their strike. Hard and gaunt, with chestnut-brown hair and deep, dark green eyes, Galt's suntanned body and guilt-free face inspire instant recognition and respect from Dagny. As an unknown worker for Taggart Transcontinental he wins Ed Willers' trust and undermines Dagny's efforts to keep capable people working. Galt does not appear, except in disguise, until halfway through the novel. He is, however, Rand's spokesperson, and in his challenge to the villains to relinquish their hold on the government, he delivers a sixty-page speech which is the philosophical crux of the story. Ironically, Dagny has thought of Galt as "the destroyer" when in actuality he is the builder of Mulligan's Valley, an ideal community in the mountains of Colorado, and the leader into a free and productive world to come. He is the culmination of Rand's effort to portray the ideal man.

Hank Rearden   A man of little self-understanding, Hank Rearden is an industrialist of tremendous ability, an inventor who perfects Rearden Metal, an alloy stronger and more flexible than steel. He shows little overt emotion; tall and gaunt, with ice-blue eyes and ash-blond hair, he gives an appearance that is strong but expressionless. A perfectionist, he looks for fault in himself, unable to understand the attitudes of those who claim they love him. He marries Lillian because he thinks she is someone to aspire to, and when she is frigid, he convinces himself that his desires are depraved. He does not understand the nature of his passion for Dagny, initially, because he is one who is convinced of the mind/body dichotomy. He showers her with lavish gifts: a pear-shaped ruby, a blue fox cape, gold bracelets and fine crystal. His guilt about his love for Dagny permits Lillian to manipulate him and cripples his ability to judge others. However, he soon becomes more self-aware and begins to rebel against his self-imposed martyrdom. In his refusal to recognize the court's right to dispose of his property without his consent, he delivers a consummate defense of capitalism. Though his feelings for Francisco d'Anconia are strained by Francisco's superficial public image, their friendship grows until Rearden finds out that Francisco had been Dagny's lover. Once he learns about Mulligan's Valley and becomes one of the strikers, he is among people who appreciate his value and who will be friends worthy of him.

CHARACTERS OF VIRTUE BUT LESSER IMPORT

Minor characters serve to reinforce Rand's themes. Though these characters do not always play significant roles in the plot, they do serve to exemplify certain virtues and/or to give aid and succor to the protagonists.

We the Living

Sasha Chernov   Sasha is a young student of history who is thrown out of the University because of his background and political views. He is Irina's fiancé, and his counterrevolutionary activity earns him exile to Siberia.

Irina Dunaev   Irina is a talented artist with a bent for satiric drawings. She is naturally loving and does not accept conventional values; she is the only one in her family who visits Kira when the rest reject her as a fallen woman. Her "sanctity of life" speech when she is about to be shipped off to sure death in Siberia is one of the keynotes of the novel.

Vasili Ivanovitch Dunaev   Once a tall, powerful man of some community stature, Vasili Ivanovitch becomes stooped and self-deluding about the future of the Communist regime. He keeps expecting Europe to intervene. Vasili is a man of great spirit and principle; he refuses to get a Soviet job or adjust to the new order. Although he tries to rationalize his son's behavior, he eventually disowns Victor when he realizes the full extent of his perfidy.

Captain Karsavin   Karsavin is one of the last leaders of the White army. Andrei encounters him in the aftermath of the battle of Perekop and a mutual respect develops. Rather than be captured by the Red Army, Karsavin commits suicide; Andrei gives him the gun.

Glieb Ilyitch Lavrov   Marisha's father is a man of the working class who spent years exiled in Siberia for fighting Czarist oppression. He refuses to be coopted by the Soviet regime and denounces it as heartily as he denounced the Czar.

Stepan Timonshenko   Timonshenko is a hard, tough sailor in the Red Baltic fleet. However, he does not lack sensitivity. When he realizes Kira and Leo's situation, he helps Kira get away and frees Leo from jail. A good friend to Andrei, and a dedicated revolutionary, he realizes early that the revolution has been perverted and that gluttonous speculators and opportunists will profit rather than the masses he fought to free. His last act is to try to protect Andrei; he sends him a letter that will safeguard him from Syerov.

Night of January 16th

Defense Attorney Stevens   A man who projects sophistication and urbane gentility, Stevens does an admirable job defending Karen Andre. In his closing argument he captures the essence of the opposing senses of life that are dramatized in the persons of Faulkner and Whitfield.

Siegurd Jungquist   Bjorn Faulkner's loyal bookkeeper, turned secretary, Jungquist has unswerving admiration for his boss. Though his devotion to Faulkner and Karen is evident, he is not a good witness for them because he proudly acknowledges that he would lie for Faulkner. He is probably the inadvertent cause of Faulkner's murder when he reveals information to Whitfield about the whereabouts of the ten million dollars Faulkner transferred to Buenos Aires.

Anthem

International 4–8818   Tall, strong, with a sense of humor and tendency to smile in a society where such behavior is not encouraged, International 4–8818 maintains an unspoken friendship with Equality 7–2521. It is a show of preference which is a sin in their brotherhood. International 4–8818 keeps his friend's secret and does not report Equality 7–2521's crime against the Council.

The Fountainhead

Henry Cameron   A cantankerous, overbearing old man who has been at the top of the field of architecture. Because he did not pay his dues to society, he is reduced to a ramshackle office and few commissions.

Still passionate about his work, though drink has made some inroads on his health, he allows Roark to work for him though he is fearful of what the powers that be will do to Roark's integrity. His philosophy of architecture is that no building should copy any other.

John Fargo   Because he admires both Gowan's Service Station and Heller's house, Fargo asks Roark to design the Fargo store which will be built on the location of a former competitor's store.

Jimmy Gowan   A man who has worked like a mule to raise enough money to build his own business, Gowan hires Roark to build his gas station. He does not care what people think.

Austen Heller   The man who gives Howard Roark his start by giving Roark $500 to open an office and a contract to build his house remains Roark's friend and supporter throughout Roark's career. Heller, a tall, broad-shouldered, square-faced man with sandy hair and calm eyes, is a writer of national stature and following, the star columnist for the *Chronicle*. In several instances he writes articles in defense of Roark; he does so during both of Roark's court cases. Heller also tries to send Roark clients and is responsible for the article that makes Roark famous. He acts as a self-appointed guardian, always warning Roark and watching out for him although, more often than not, Roark doesn't listen.

Kent Lansing   Lansing comes into Roark's life out of the blue and gets Roark a commission to build the Aquitania, a luxurious hotel on Central Park South. Lansing is a man of integrity who knows quality and will fight to have what he wants. He understands the psychology of boards and unions and corporations which he equates with "other chain gangs," and because he knows what he wants while others don't, he gets what he wants.

Steven Mallory   A sculptor of heroic figures, Mallory has been so buffeted by life that he is reduced to creating plaster baby plaques for dime stores. Mallory is, at first, too bitter to believe that Roark wants him to create a sculpture for the Stoddard Temple for no reason other than the quality of his work. Mallory tries to kill Ellsworth Toohey and though he will not disclose the reason in court, he later explains to Roark the nature of Toohey's treachery. Roark and Mallory become friends and Mallory becomes an unknowing intermediary in Howard and Dominique's relationship. Mallory is passionate, high-strung, and an artist of great ability; his talent is immediately appreciated by Roark, Toohey and Wynand. His statue of Dominique, in a nude attitude of exaltation, representing the heroic human spirit, is the centerpiece for the Stoddard Temple.

Atlas Shrugged

In *Atlas Shrugged* most of the able and virtuous people join the "strike of the mind" and become deserters. Some live on the outside, doing menial jobs, thereby not allowing the moochers and the leeches to utilize their brainpower. Some move into Mulligan's Valley on a full-time basis. A few in this list are good people who have not found their way to the strikers, but find themselves unable to function in the collectivist and bureaucratic society.

Hugh Akston   A philosophy professor at Patrick Henry University who functions as a father figure for Francisco, Ragnar, and John Galt, Akston is one of the last advocates of reason in the halls of academe, a believer that contradictions do not exist. He quits academia and works in a diner when he is not in the valley.

Jeff Allen   A skilled lathe operator who cannot find an honest job and therefore becomes a bum, Allen is put in charge of a stranded train by Dagny. He tells Dagny the story of Twentieth Century Motor Company.

Calvin Atwood   The owner of Atwood Light and Power Company of New York City becomes the owner of Atwood Leather Goods Company in Mulligan's Valley.

Bill Brent   The chief dispatcher for the Colorado Division of Taggart Transcontinental warns Mitchum about the possible tunnel disaster, refuses to sign the order to send the Comet through the tunnel, and quits rather than be forced to do what he knows is wrong.

Tom Colby   The rolling mill foreman and head of the Rearden Steel Workers Union, a company union, quits when Directive 10–289 is declared.

Dan Conway   A square and solid man near fifty who runs the Phoenix/Durango railroad, Conway is Taggart's chief competitor in Colorado until the Anti-dog-eat-dog Rule is declared. Then he retires to his ranch in Arizona.

Ken Danagger   The owner of Danagger Coal in Pennsylvania started as a miner. In his fifties at the time of the collectivist takeover, he tries to help Rearden and is indicted with him for subverting government orders. Though he loves his work and his mines, he retires and leaves the mines to no one.

Quentin Daniels   Daniels is a young physicist who has refused to work for Dr. Stadler at the State Science Institute, but agrees to try to help Dagny reconstruct the motor. He resigns his job with her because he doesn't want the motor to be used in the service of tyranny. It is when she is trying to keep him from disappearing that Dagny crashes into the valley.

Richard Halley   The composer whose heroic music is the theme song for the novel, Halley is a composer of intrepid, rebellious, and inspirational music. He achieves acclaim after many years of struggle, but retires the day after the success of his opera, *Phaethon*.

Lawrence Hammond   The last producer of good cars and trucks in the outer world, Hammond, the owner of Hammond Car Company in Colorado, retires to run the grocery store in Mulligan's Valley.

Mrs. William Hasting   The widow of the man who was chief engineer of the laboratory at Twentieth Century Motors is a dignified and serene woman who gives Dagny the clue which leads to Hugh Akston.

Dr. Thomas Hendricks   A great surgeon who retires and vanishes after the socialization of medicine, Dr. Hendricks treats Dagny after her crash into Mulligan's Valley.

Gwen Ives   Hank Rearden's calm and efficient secretary breaks down in tears when she hears of the passing of the Equalization of Opportunity Bill.

Owen Kellogg   The first dropout that Dagny encounters, Kellogg is a young engineer who was assistant to the manager of Taggart Terminal in New York. He refuses her offer of a promotion. They meet on the frozen train and then again in Mulligan's Valley.

Pat Logan   The engineer of the Taggart Comet on the Nebraska Division wins the lottery to drive the first run of the John Galt line on rails of Rearden Metal.

Kay Ludlow   Kay is an unusual beauty who was a movie star. She is married to Ragnar Danneskjöld and waits in the valley while Ragnar risks his life. She performs plays there by authors unknown to the outside world.

Roger Marsh   Marsh has owned a factory of electrical appliances near the town of Marshville. He tries not to desert, but eventually does without leaving a word for Nielsen. He grows cabbage in Mulligan's Valley.

Ray McKim   A large, grinning and confident young fireman, McKim works the first run of the John Galt line.

Dick McNamara   Among the best contractors in the country, McNamara is one of the first of Dagny's business associates to walk out. He quits with a pile of contracts and a three-year waiting list of clients.

Michael "Midas" Mulligan   Though he looks like a truck driver, Mulligan is the richest man in the country. He owns the valley where all the able and competent have gathered to build their own Atlantis and await the downfall of the collectivist state. The Valley bears his name and he runs a bank there where all exchange is done in gold.

Judge Narragansett   Once the judge of the Superior Court of Illinois, Judge Narragansett runs a chicken and dairy farm in Mulligan's Valley. He quit the bench when a court of appeals reversed his ruling that those who earn are more entitled than one whose only claim is need. He would not uphold injustice.

Ted Nielsen   Ted Nielsen, the owner of Nielsen Motors, quits and disappears when the John Galt line is closed. In Mulligan's Valley he works as a lumberjack.

Dwight Sanders   A maker of good airplanes, Dwight Sanders, who owned Sanders Aircraft, becomes a hog farmer and plane attendant in the Valley.

Andrew Stockton   One of the people whose profession does not change in the Valley, Andrew Stockton has the Stockton Foundry there as he had it in Stockton, Colorado. Stockton is an eager competitor who is anxious to hire the sort of people who might one day be his most able competition.

Mr. Ward   Mr. Ward is the fourth generation of his family to run Ward Harvester Company in Minnesota. It is a small, solid company and Mr. Ward is ready to sell at a loss if it means keeping his doors open. He comes to Hank Rearden because he cannot get steel and Rearden gets it for him.

Ellis Wyatt   Young, quick-tempered, and able, Ellis Wyatt is in the business of reviving old oil wells and making them produce again. A loner, he invites Dagny and Hank to dinner and to spend the night at his home at the conclusion of the first run of the John Galt line. After the crippling directives are issued, he destroys Wyatt Oil and vanishes into the Valley.

THE ARCHVILLAINOUS ANTAGONISTS

Just as Rand's goal in writing Romantic fiction is to portray the ideal man and thereby accomplish the didactic purpose of illustrating desirable human behavior, so she parallels the lesson by illustrating through her antagonists and villains those kinds of people and behaviors that are most repulsive and detrimental to human happiness. She creates two types of negative characters: those who are weak or ignorant and thereby impede their own and the progress of others and those who actively choose to do evil. In this category of the Archvillainous Antagonists, I have included only characters of the latter type. The archvillains are individuals who seek power, a power they use to do ill, even ultimately to themselves.

We the Living

Victor Dunaev   An opportunist of the first order, Victor Dunaev has no loyalty or honor. He uses everyone. He marries Marisha because he thinks her proletariat background will help him in the party. When that is not enough to get him the job he wants, he turns in his sister and her fiancé for counterrevolutionary activities to prove his loyalty to the party. He looks like a matinee idol with black wavy hair and burning black eyes, and he uses his charms solely to advance himself.

Pavel Syerov   Though he stayed home with a cold during the opening battles of the revolution, Pavel Syerov portrays himself as a true revolutionary. He is a bit of a dandy who sees himself as something of a lady's man, but Pavel's use of Comrade Sonia to further his party aims backfires when she becomes pregnant and blackmails him into marrying her. While spouting the party line, Syerov secretly backs the black-market speculations of Karp Morozov and Leo Kovalensky. His party connections save him when his black-market dealings are uncovered; his hypocrisy continues when he uses Andrei's funeral as an opportunity for self-aggrandizement.

Night of January 16th

John Graham Whitfield   Extremely wealthy, impeccably dressed, and distinguished looking, Whitfield is a man who is used to getting what he wants. President of Whitfield National Bank, he extends a ten million dollar loan to Bjorn Faulkner to buy Faulkner for his daughter. The testimonies of "Guts" Regan and Siegurd Jungquist indicate that when Whitfield realized that Faulkner had extorted his money and was planning a fake suicide, he killed Faulkner and burned the body.

Nancy Lee Faulkner   Young, beautiful, and blonde, Nancy Lee Whitfield Faulkner is, by her testimony, a bereaved widow. Other testimony, however, indicates that she bought Bjorn Faulkner, well aware that he did not care for her, and that she had tried to force him to give up Karen Andre.

Anthem

The World Council of Scholars   Supposedly a council of the wisest of all the lands, the World Council of Scholars will not accept the gift of electricity because it was not discovered collectively and also because it may ruin the Department of Candles. They teach that the earth is flat and that the sun revolves around it. Their response to new discovery and invention is to order its destruction and the punishment of the discoverer.

The Fountainhead

Peter Keating   "I am a parasite," Keating tells Roark, and in that statement of self-recognition aptly characterizes his villainy and his weakness. Because he wants to feel superior, Keating blackmails, plagiarizes, and beguiles his way to the top of his field. His natural attributes of dark good looks and easy popularity are used to ingratiate himself with his superiors. He moves easily from star of the student body at the Stanton Institute of Technology to rising young architect in the firm of Francon & Heyer by becoming whatever people want him to be. He marries Dominique, whom he does not love, for the prestige, and thereby fails Katie, the only woman he does love. He then sells Dominique for the Stoneridge commission. By the age of thirty-nine he is a miserable has-been, and though he understands the nature of his betrayal of self, he is too weak and dependent to change. His presence at Roark's trial has little impact because there is no being left in the shell of his body.

Ellsworth Monkton Toohey   Rand's most self-aware villain, Toohey knows how to control people and chooses the role of soul-collector over other courses in life. His method is to find weaknesses and play on them. An aunt who sees through him says, "You're a maggot, Elsie. . . . You feed on sores." "Then I'll never starve," is his reply. By making humans feel small, guilty and low, he helps kill their integrity. All this is done by preaching selflessness and egolessness and destroying people's hierarchy of values. Toohey's desire is to be the great leveler, to extinguish all desire to excel. Fragile-looking, like a "chicken just emerging from the egg," he uses a sonorous, velvet-like voice to manipulate people. Though he is often quite direct and tells many that he is dangerous, no one takes him seriously—they assume he is joking. Toohey succeeds in winning his case to make Wynand rehire him on the *Banner*, but Wynand stops the presses on the day of Toohey's return. Toohey then goes to work for the *Courier*, a prestigious paper, and continues his manipulative ways.

Atlas Shrugged

Dr. Floyd Ferris   His dark good looks, six-foot frame and moustache make him a Valentino type, but his actions are more like the Grand Inquisitor. He invents the Ferris Persuader to torture without killing. His is a theory of control by guilt, and when that doesn't work, blackmail is his fallback technique. He uses the resources of the Science Institute to deride reason and logic in his book *Why Do You Think You Think?* He uses Stadler, at first with feigned respect, but then with contempt when he knows he is in control.

Wesley Mouch   Mouch begins as Rearden's man in Washington, but quickly betrays Rearden to become the Assistant Coordinator for the Bureau of Economic Planning and National Resources. James Taggart engineers the double cross. Squarish and pale looking with a petulant lower lip and egg-like eyes, Mouch never smiles. He rises quickly in Washington, advanced by mediocrity-loving people. When his programs don't work, he whines for greater powers. He pushes Directive 10–289 to achieve stasis and becomes the Economic Director of the country.

Lillian Rearden   Hank Rearden's wife is thought of as a glacial and classical beauty, full of gaiety and liveliness. It is all outward show; her eyes are lifeless. She wants her husband to make her happy, but she doesn't know what it will take. She does not appreciate Hank's worth, condescendingly grants him his marital rights as if they were shameful, and displays his gift of a bracelet of Rearden Metal against diamonds to make it look tacky. She delivers her husband over to his enemies and delights in being instrumental in taking Rearden Metal away from him.

Dr. Robert Stadler   Once recognized as the greatest physicist of his time, Dr. Stadler compromises his integrity to be freed from material concerns. As the young head of the physics department at Patrick Henry University, he is Francisco's, Ragnar's, and John Galt's teacher, but he loses their respect despite his abilities. He allows himself to be used by Dr. Ferris, rationalizing all the while. When he has the opportunity to denounce the State Science Institute, he is too cowardly to do so. Because of his genius, he is the guiltiest of the villains.

James Taggart   Dagny's brother and president of Taggart Transcontinental looks near fifty though he is only thirty-nine. He is wan, petulant, and irritable, and his greatest fear is that he will be held responsible for anything. He is a parasite of the first order, always relying on Dagny to get him out of trouble, attempting to ride Francisco's coattails to riches. He marries Cherryl because he thinks she is beneath him and will therefore adore him. He and Lillian Rearden connive to keep Rearden in line. In his desire to kill John Galt, he finally comes face to face with his hatred of existence.

SECONDARY UNWORTHY OR VILLAINOUS CHARACTERS

Whether they are aiding and abetting the villains in their rise to power or personifying and perpetuating the evils of collectivism, altruism, or mysticism, Rand's secondary unworthy and villainous characters swarm over her literary canvas like Hogarth's inhabitants of Gin Lane or Breughel's villagers. Rand's satire of and invective against a large part of society are often capsulized in her mini-portraits of secondary characters. The number and variety of these lesser beings increase as her message became clearer and more encompassing. By the time she wrote *Atlas Shrugged*, the list included representatives from such far-flung areas as train engineering, composing, and sociology.

We the Living

Galina Petrova Argounovna   Kira's mother is a completely adaptable person. Though she denounces communism privately, she spouts the party line in front of party members. She throws Kira out when she finds Kira has been sleeping with Leo, but later calls marriage a bourgeois prejudice. Eventually, she becomes totally acculturated and teaches in a labor school.

Lydia Argounovna   Kira's older sister is a talented pianist who takes comfort in spirituality. She is conventional, small-spirited, and generally unhappy, but she doesn't understand why.

Comrade Bitiuk   The office manager at the House of the Peasant and Kira's boss is a tall, thin, stern woman who is in total sympathy with the Communist regime.

Rita Eksler   Audacious and sexually aggressive, Rita is a woman who goes through three husbands.

Vava Nilovskaia   The daughter of a gynecologist who prospers under the new Soviet regime, Vava tries to retain some of the gaiety of earlier times. She is in love with Victor, but when she finds him with Marisha, she first makes love to Leo and then marries Kolya Smiatkin on the rebound.

Karp Karpovitch Morozov (Koko)   A large, blond, heavyset man who engages in illegal speculation, Koko keeps Tonia as a mistress and uses

Leo as a front man for his speculative business ventures because Leo is the perfect fall guy.

Antonina Pavlovna Platoshkina (Tonia)   A large, garish woman who meets Leo at the sanatorium, Tonia is Koko's mistress and later keeps Leo as a gigolo.

Comrade Sonia Presniakova   Ambitious and aggressive, Comrade Sonia has her mind set on marrying Pavel Syerov. She accomplishes this by becoming pregnant and then exerting subtle political blackmail. She has political savvy and uses it to attain party power.

Kolya Smiatkin   Hopelessly and doggedly devoted to Vava, Smiatkin is young, blond, and chubby. He acts as vice-secretary of the club library without pay in order to avoid losing his job.

Night of January 16th

District Attorney Flint   In his closing argument Karen Andre's prosecutor calls for the jury to uphold common standards and crush the concept of man as conqueror.

Magda Swanson   The Faulkner family housekeeper for thirty-eight years is plain, religious, and middle-aged, and hates Karen. She thinks Karen is a sinful and shameless woman and testifies against her at the trial.

The Fountainhead

Mr. and Mrs. Dale Ainsworth   This couple owns the late Renaissance and gray granite home which Peter Keating designed; Dominique ridicules it in her column.

Allen   The slot man, head of the copy desk at the *Banner*, is fired by Wynand for disobeying orders.

Athelstan Beasley   The head of the Arts Ball and general wit of the world of architecture, Beasley writes a column and organizes social events; he does little designing and building, however.

Caleb Bradley   A crooked entrepreneur who sells 200 percent of the Monadnock Valley summer resort project, Bradley chooses Roark as its architect because he thinks that Roark will assure its failure.

Sally Brent   The *Banner* resident sob sister breaks Wynand's ban on writing about Mrs. Gail Wynand; Brent writes a treacly account of the marriage, which gets her fired. She then writes an exposé of Wynand's love life for the *New Frontier*.

Dwight Carson   Though he begins as a writer of great integrity, Carson is bought by Gail Wynand and forced to write for the masses. He becomes a dipsomaniac.

Lancelot Clokey   A foreign correspondent who has written a best seller about his personal adventures in foreign countries, Clokey uses significant world events as a backdrop for recounting his sordid experiences; only Toohey's advocacy makes the book sell.

Lois Cook   The author of *The Gallant Gallstone* is a thirty-seven-year-old woman who likes to say she is sixty-four. She has no delusions about the quality of her work, but argues that worth is not important, that words should be freed from the stranglehold of reason. A large, unkempt woman who lives on inherited money, she wants to build the ugliest house in New York because anyone can build a nice-looking house. She is part of Toohey's inner circle.

Tim Davis   Peter Keating's first step on his rise in Francon & Heyer is to supplant Tim Davis as favored draftsman. Tim allows Peter to do much of his work; Tim's energies are devoted to his romance and subsequent marriage. He is frequently late for work and soon gets fired.

Dean of the Stanton Institute of Technology   Though he perfunctorily tries to soften Roark's expulsion from Stanton, the Dean realizes that his advice has no impact on Roark. Horrified at Roark's attitude, the Dean calls Roark a dangerous man.

Neil Dumont   A poor designer, but a man with aristocratic connections, Dumont becomes Peter Keating's best friend. When Guy Francon retires, Dumont becomes Keating's partner.

Mrs. Dunlop   A young and attractive woman whom Peter Keating influences into hiring Stengel as the architect for her home. This commission gives Stengel the start he needs to leave Francon & Heyer, thereby moving Keating up to the position of chief designer.

Falk   A copyreader for the *Banner*, Falk is fired along with Allen, Harding, and Toohey.

Jules Fougler   The drama critic for the *Banner* and one of Toohey's inner circle, Fougler is a saggy and cynical man who believes that the dramatist is irrelevant and the daily life of the common man can just as readily be critiqued for its artistic points. He decides to make Ike's wretched play, *No Skin off Your Ass*, a hit, just because it is such a poor play.

Mrs. Gillespie Tall, toothy, dripping in diamonds, this woman can't believe that Ellsworth Toohey can be a radical because he is not dirty.

Mr. Harding The sixty-year-old managing editor of the *Banner* is fired by Wynand for allowing Toohey's anti-Roark article to be printed. Harding's wife writes a response published under his name in *New Frontiers*.

Lucius N. Heyer A collector of old porcelain who looks as if he had just been bled, Heyer is the last of a dissipated old bloodline. He is Guy Francon's partner, chosen for his monied connections. He is generally ineffectual in the firm and leaves his share to Peter.

Constance (Kiki) Holcombe A small, perky and vivacious woman who tries to look younger than her forty-two years, Kiki collects famous people in her architects' salon. She has made a career of entertaining.

Ralston Holcombe The president of the Architect's Guild of America is a round, pink man with a mane of white hair who dresses outlandishly and affects a temperament of artistic bravura. His specialty is state buildings and monuments and he is obsessed with Renaissance style.

Ike The author of *No Skin off Your Ass*, which is produced under the title *No Skin off Your Nose*, is a talentless twenty-six-year-old playwright who has written eleven unproduced plays. He doesn't see why talent ought to be a factor in writing plays.

Mr. Nathaniel Janss Bullied by Austen Heller into giving Roark a chance at a commission for the Janss-Stuart Real Estate Company office building, Janss agrees with Roark's arguments for not building with unnecessary ornamentation. However, he cannot hold out against his board of directors.

Mrs. Louisa Keating Peter's mother is the prototype of the self-sacrificing and directing mother who influences her son away from art and into architecture, away from the woman he loves and toward a woman with more social prominence. She does not understand why Peter ends up such a miserable man.

Vincent Knowlton One of Peter Keating's crowd, Knowlton is characterized by Dominique as innocuous.

Eve Layton A beautiful woman whose main desire is to be avant-garde, Eve is a very athletic woman, yet willing to make careless intellectual leaps as well. Her husband hates her.

Mitchell Layton A pouting, obnoxious young man who feels guilty about his inheritance, Layton slouches about mouthing ideas that espouse more societal regulation and less choice. He buys part of the *Banner* and helps Toohey undermine Wynand.

Robert Mundy   Sent by Austen Heller to Roark, Mundy is obsessed with recreating for himself a copy of the mansion of the county in which he grew up in poverty. Roark cannot convince him to build a monument to his own rather than someone else's success.

Eugene Pettingill   In his seventies and most unattractive, Pettingill is one of the conventional architects who speaks out against Roark's work.

Jessica Pratt   A woman whose guiding principle is unselfishness, Jessica has dedicated her life to her sister, Renee Slottern.

Gordon J. Prescott   Tall, tanned, blond, and athletic-looking, with the demeanor of a university man, Prescott always wears turtlenecks. He keeps Roark waiting two and a half hours for their first appointment. Though he writes an article about his encouragement of talented newcomers, Prescott's idea of originality is reproduction of old forms into new purposes. He calls his approach utilitarian and pragmatic.

June Sanborn   The nineteen-year-old daughter of the Whitford Sanborns has romantic preconceptions about architects, and when Roark does not respond to her flirtation, proclaims her hatred for the house he designs.

Whitford Sanborn   Because he has been so satisfied with an office building that Henry Cameron designed for him, Whitford Sanborn takes Cameron's advice and contracts with Roark to build him a country home. Though he loves the modern home that Roark builds for him, he is too weak to hold out against his wife's refusal to live in it.

Mrs. Whitford Sanborn   A woman who cares more about what her friends think of her home and appearances than anything else, Whitford Sanborn's wife tries to sabotage Roark's plans at every turn. When the house is built, she refuses to live in it.

Alvah Scarret   Though he looks like a kindly country doctor, and though he had been totally devoted to Gail Wynand and the *Banner*, Scarret aids Toohey in his takeover plans. He is editor-in-chief and Dominique's boss when she works at the *Banner*. Vehemently opposed to Wynand's marrying Dominique, he tries to convince Gail that he should not marry her. When Dominique goes to Howard, Scarret is the one who takes the news to Wynand and insists on a divorce. He then uses the paper to create the image of Wynand as the victim of a depraved woman with whom he was madly infatuated.

Homer Slottern   A man who is ashamed of his ownership of three department stores, Slottern feels that he has neglected his spiritual growth.

He dresses ostentatiously, believes theories are nonsense, and joins the group that buys part of the *Banner* in order to undermine Wynand.

Renee Slottern   Homer's wife is a vacant and naive woman to whose upbringing her sister has dedicated her life.

John Erik Snyte   The head of an architecture firm which includes one architect for each style, Snyte hires Howard to be the modernist. After each architect submits a plan, Snyte makes an amalgam of their work. Snyte bastardizes Roark's plans for Austen Heller's house and then fires Howard when he corrects the plans in Heller's presence. He tries to rehire Roark when he finds out that Heller has given him the commission.

Hopton Stoddard   A smiling little man who has taken refuge in religion as he grows older, Stoddard plans a nondenominational temple to leave as a monument to faith. He is totally under the influence of Ellsworth Toohey and files suit against Roark for breach of contract and malpractice when the temple does not reflect his vision of faith.

Joel Sutton   A badminton-playing, "smiling ball of meat," Sutton lacks any discrimination—he loves everything and everyone. At first he chooses Roark as his architect because Enright has, but then he takes the commission away because Dominique suggests that Keating would be a more popular choice.

Mrs. Mary Toohey   Ellsworth's mother loves him from the moment he is born because he is so uninspiring of love. She is an erratic woman who goes through a number of religions, but idolizes only Ellsworth. She constantly nags his father to get things for Ellsworth.

Gus Webb   A crude-talking, tough, socially ungracious architect who leads the "We Don't Read Wynand" movement, Webb is the vicious kind of individual who is sorry there were no people in the Cortlandt project when Roark blew it up.

Atlas Shrugged

Mayor Bascom   Bascom is the dingily dressed, pear-shaped, and unprincipled mayor of the dying town of Rome, Wisconsin. He tells Dagny part of the story of Twentieth Century Motors.

Luke Beal   The fireman of the doomed Comet, Beal is one who thought his superiors knew what they were doing.

Dr. Blodgett   A young, fattish scientist, Blodgett is the man who pulls the lever to demonstrate Project X.

Orren Boyle   A large, loud man with slit-like eyes, Boyle is the head of Associated Steel. He makes a fortune with government money. Because his business is not successful, he wants to limit Hank Rearden and make the most of government subsidies. He also pushes to open patents so that he can produce Rearden Metal. When Rearden quits, he has a nervous breakdown.

Laura Bradford   A movie actress who made her way to the top by sleeping with bureaucrats, Laura Bradford is Kip Chalmers' mistress.

Kip Chalmers   A second-rater from the semi-powerful ranks of bureaucrats, Kip Chalmers is running for the legislature of California.

Emma "Ma" Chalmers   After her son's death in the Taggart Tunnel disaster, Ma Chalmers becomes something of a celebrity. A mystic and a Buddhist, Ma tries to convert the country to a soybean diet, a disastrous scheme which ruins the wheat harvest.

Balph Eubank   The literary leader of the period is one who believes that "plot is a primitive vulgarity in literature." Eubank also feels that the essence of life is defeat and suffering, and therefore that is what literature should reveal.

Señor Rodrigo Gonzalez   A man who looks like a killer, Rodrigo is famous for his parties. He is the diplomatic representative of Chile who joined the regime that nationalized his property.

Señora Gonzalez   An asset to her husband because she helps influence people in his favor, Señora Gonzalez has the reputation of being a beauty due to the frenetic quality of energy she displays.

Tinky Holloway   A rat-faced, slim and slouching man who is described in tennis imagery, Holloway is one of the influence peddlers along with Taggart, Mouch, Morrison, Meigs, Ferris, and Thompson. He explains the Steel Unification plan to Rearden.

Lee Hunsacker   A worn-out has-been at forty-two, Hunsacker blames everyone but himself for his failures. He heads the Amalgamated Service which takes over Twentieth Century Motors and brings suit against Midas Mulligan for not loaning him money. His is the suit that precipitates Mulligan's and Narragansett's withdrawal from a looter's society.

Fred Kinnan   A racketeer who heads Amalgamated Labor of America, Kinnan is one of the most honest of the looters. He does not pretend that he is doing anything else. He calls the actions of the government an "anti-industrial revolution" and points out the pitfalls of their actions or lack of action.

Gilbert Keith-Worthing   A seventy-year-old British novelist whose world fame consists of books that haven't been read. His line is that since there is no such thing as freedom, then people should not mind the tyranny of a dictatorship. Flabby, obese, and cynical, he is Kip Chalmers' guest on the Comet.

Paul Larkin   An unsuccessful man who takes advantage of his friendship with the Rearden family, Larkin takes over the Rearden ore mines under the Equalization Bill. Though he assures Rearden that his ownership is only a technicality and that he will continue providing ore, he doesn't. Short, plump, and boyish at fifty-three, he is one who wheedles and whines and rationalizes his failures.

Eugene Lawson   When the Community Bank of Madison that he heads goes bankrupt, Lawson gets a job in Washington, D.C., with the Bureau of Economic Planning and National Resources. He preaches the line that personal goals don't matter and that it is everyone's social obligation to produce. He calls the mind corrupt and declares that it is the Age of Love rather than Reason.

Mort Liddy   A composer of old-fashioned movie scores, Liddy also popularizes and mangles Halley's concerto to win an award as best movie score of the year.

Clifton Locey   A master at not taking the responsibility for any action, Locey is a friend of Jim Taggart's who is put in as Operating Vice President when Dagny quits. He knows little and cares nothing about the railroad; his only goal is to please Taggart and Washington.

Cuffy Meigs   An ignorant, uncouth lout, of bulging girth and nasal voice, Meigs is the Director of Unification. He takes over Project X and drunkenly and stupidly pulls the wrong lever on the xylophone.

David Mitchum   Because the good men have quit and because he has pull, Mitchum becomes the superintendent of the Colorado Division of Taggart Transcontinental, but he shirks his decision-making responsibilities.

Chick Morrison   A nonentity who serves as Morale Conditioner, Morrison resigns after John Galt's speech.

Horace Bussby Mowen   Though he is president of Amalgamated Switch and Signal Company of Connecticut, Mowen won't make switches of Rearden Metal because the people don't like it. When public opinion changes, so does his. He believes in the Equalization of Opportunity Bill and is the show industrialist for the government.

Ben Nealy   Soft, bulky and sullen, Nealy is a contractor who replaces McNamara. He complains about Wyatt, though Wyatt takes care of problems that should be attended to by Nealy.

Betty Pope   A member of one of the best families, Betty Pope is a homely woman who sleeps with Jim Taggart.

Dr. Potter   As representative from the State Science Institute, Potter attempts to discourage Rearden's marketing of Rearden Metal. When he fails, he attempts to buy it.

Dr. Simon Pritchett   The author of *The Metaphysical Contradictions of the Universe* preaches the doctrine that human beings are just chemistry and biology and everything is a matter of opinion. His premise is that "Logic is a primitive vulgarity of philosophy."

Mrs. Rearden   Hank's mother is a nagging, critical, reproachful woman who only knows how to take. She does not appreciate her son's abilities and seeks to keep him bound by guilt. Her definition of virtue is giving to the undeserving.

Philip Rearden   Rather than appreciating his brother Hank's charity, Philip Rearden lives in Hank's home and criticizes him. A sickly, tired man, he works for organizations and then spies on his brother for the government.

Joe Scott   Though he has broken the safety rules and has been fired from other jobs, Scott becomes the engineer for Taggart because of his friendship with Fred Kinnan. He goes to work drunk and is the engineer for the Comet disaster.

Bertram Scudder   The editor of *The Future* magazine, Scudder writes nasty articles about Hank Rearden. He is the broadcaster on the radio program Dagny uses to denounce the government for their blackmailing of Hank Rearden. His tone is an attempt to sound "cynical, skeptical, superior, and hysterical together."

Claude Slagenhop   The president of Friends for Global Progress, Slagenhop believes that need is the only consideration. A collectivist through and through, he thinks that there is no source for public opinion, only the collective instinct of the collective mind.

Gerald Starnes   Once the heir to Twentieth Century Motors, Starnes is found in a flophouse, willing to sell his name for a drink. With his sister, he had attempted to institute a collectivist system at the factory.

Ivy Starnes   When she and her brothers inherit Twentieth Century Motors, Ivy Starnes institutes a plan to run it by the precept, "From each according to his ability, to each according to his need." When the plan ruins the plant, she retires to Eastern religions and a foul-smelling Mississippi bungalow.

Mr. Thompson   A nondescript, wilted looking man, Thompson schemes his way to becoming head of state. He is a product of chance who is willing to be flexible about everything and whose code of belief is that everyone is open to a deal.

Lester Tuck   Kip Chalmers' press agent, Tuck is an ex-attorney who used to represent shoplifters.

Clem Weatherby   Washington's man on the Taggart Transcontinental board, Weatherby is an influence trader. He is the one who suggests that Taggart keep Rearden in line.

NEUTRAL OR METAMORPHOSING CHARACTERS

There are few characters who are presented neutrally in Rand's works because by her moral premises, humans all have choices and therefore are responsible for their actions or inaction. Most of the neutral characters in her early works are functionaries for plot purposes; by the time Rand writes *Atlas Shrugged* she has classified almost every character in either a positive or a negative category. Classifying Eddie Willers, however, does present a problem. He is neither neutral nor metamorphosing. Though there is reason to believe that Rand meant him to be a positive character, he never does learn the lesson the other heroes learn. He is left stranded on a frozen train as his punishment.

Besides the neutral individuals, this section also includes the metamorphosing characters—those who begin in one group and then through reevaluation or experience move to the opposite camp. They are few, but still possible in Rand's perception of character.

We the Living

Alexander Dimitrievitch Argounov   Once the owner of a granite mansion and a textile factory, the father of the Argounov family is reduced by Soviet nationalization to a bookkeeping job. He is a caring but ineffectual man.

Acia Dunaev   Victor's and Irina's little sister is young and bratty.

Maria (Marussia) Petrovna Dunaev   Sallow and sickly looking, the mother of the Dunaev family was once a great beauty, but due to poor medical care dies hemorrhaging and coughing.

Marina Marisha Lavrova   Though she begins as a not-too-bright, slovenly member of Komsomol, The Communist Union of Youth, who takes over one of Leo and Kira's rooms through Victor's influence, Marisha, who marries Victor, is kind to his father and sneaks help to Irina and Sasha against Victor's wishes.

Night of January 16th

James Chandler   New York Police Department's handwriting expert is a precise and dignified man who testifies that Faulkner's suicide note is not forged.

Court Bailiff and Court Clerk   They perform their appropriate functions in court.

Judge Heath   The judge of the case of the People of the State of New York vs. Karen Andre presides in a straightforward and impartial manner.

John Hutchins   The shy, nervous watchman of the Faulkner Building testifies to letting Karen Andre, Bjorn Faulkner, and two other men into the building on the night of January 16th.

Dr. Kirkland   The elderly and kindly medical examiner testifies to the condition of the body presumed to be Bjorn Faulkner.

Elmer Sweeney   The police inspector who investigates the possible murder/suicide of Bjorn Faulkner is awed by the perfumed water in the bathroom of Karen's penthouse.

Homer Van Fleet   A private investigator hired by Nancy Lee Faulkner to follow Bjorn Faulkner, Van Fleet testifies to what he saw on the night of January 16th; he saw Karen Andre push a body over the parapet of her penthouse.

The Fountainhead

Miss Cameron   Henry Cameron's sister is a meek, elderly, emotionless woman who assumes his care when Cameron collapses.

Guy Francon   Though he is first pictured as a middle-aged, self-satisfied architect who made his name by designing the Frink National Bank Building, a miasma of columns, frills, and furbelows, Francon begins to question his values. At first he represents what Peter Keating strives to be, but then he rejects the actions of his fellow architects during the Stoddard trial. Initially he is made uncomfortable by his daughter Dominique, but during her divorce from Wynand, Francon invites her to stay with him and provides support and approval.

Catherine Halsey (Katie)   In 1921 when she comes to live with her uncle Ellsworth Toohey, Catherine is young and uncomplicated, flush with the expectation of a glowing future. Plain and a bit clumsy, she nevertheless makes Peter Keating feel wonderful as they fall in love and plan marriage. With the destruction of her dreams, she becomes first a bitter and then a petty, take-charge person who is indifferent to Peter and has obliterated thoughts of the past. Katie is one of the few Rand characters who move from positive to negative.

Richard Sanborn   Though he is considered a drunken wastrel, Whitford Sanborn's son has enough judgment to appreciate the house Roark builds and to insist on living there.

Ted Shlinker   Peter Keating's competition for outstanding student at Stanton Institute of Technology is outdistanced by Peter in the final year.

Claude Stengel   A small, bony, angular man who cannot be bought by friendship, Stengel, who does all of Francon's designing, is Keating's second step on the ladder up the Francon & Heyer hierarchy. Stengel correctly assesses Keating's perfidy.

Mr. Weidler   A friend of Richard Sanborn's who is on the board of Metropolitan Bank Company, Weidler gets the bank board to accept Roark's drawing although he gives in to the condition of a classical facade.

Atlas Shrugged

Cherryl Brooks Taggart   When she meets James Taggart, who she thinks is the unsung hero of Taggart Transcontinental, Cherryl is nineteen, starry-eyed, and works in a dime store. She is so enthralled with Jim's attention that she drowns her doubts. Initially hostile to Dagny, she learns slowly and painfully that Dagny is what she thought Jim was. She apologizes to Dagny, but does not have the strength to cope with the horrors she encounters and thus runs through the darkness over a parapet to her death.

Wet Nurse (Tony)   Put into Rearden Mills by Washington to act as an enforcer of government policies, Wet Nurse, the name given him by the steel workers, starts as a cynic who does not believe in absolutes. He comes to admire Rearden, and tells Rearden to do as he pleases and that he will juggle the books so Washington won't know. He eventually gives his life to protect Rearden's Mills.

Eddie Willers   The Special Assistant to the Vice President of Operations of Taggart Transcontinental is a retainer of the Taggart family as his forefathers were before him. Fair, direct and fiercely loyal to Dagny and Taggart Transcontinental, Eddie is culpable in two areas: he discloses Dagny's private business to an unknown railroad worker who turns out to be John Galt; he cannot quit and continues to let the leeches use his abilities.

CHAPTER 4

The Nonfiction

Rand's fiction brought her to the attention of many young intellectuals for whom she filled a need that had been starved by the prevailing existential, relativistic, and Marxist philosophies. With *Atlas Shrugged* she enhanced and completed what she had accomplished on a lesser scale in *The Fontainhead*: John Galt is her portrayal of an ideal man who is all that Howard Roark was and more; not only does she provide the portrait of one ideal man, but she embellishes it with her depiction of three others on a similar scale; to complete her ideal cast of characters, she creates the ideal woman, Dagny Taggart. Rand had achieved the goal she set for herself as a writer. Furthermore, she created for these ideal characters the opportunity to fulfill the ultimate fantasy: righting all the world's wrongs. After *Atlas Shrugged*, Rand published no more fiction. She had fulfilled her destiny as an imaginative writer; she had created an ideal world peopled with ideal characters. *Atlas Shrugged*, like the Bible, remains the main myth (I define myth as the narrative which embodies the dogma and values of a particular group) to which the subsequent philosophical essays continually refer.

The second stage of Rand's career as a writer developed naturally as a result of the interest her works of fiction aroused in readers for whom the thought content was as, if not more, important than the plot and characters. Of course there are many readers whose appetites are quite satisfied by the exciting stories and whose interest does not go beyond the fiction. In the interim between the publication of *The Fountainhead* and *Atlas Shrugged*, Rand had established a close relationship with Nathaniel and Barbara Branden. That association had a significant effect on the direction of her writing career. Her informal meetings with them to discuss the larger implications of her philosophy led, after the publication of *Atlas Shrugged*, to the formation of classes by which more students could be introduced to Objectivism. Under the auspices of the Nathaniel Branden Lectures the first course, "The Basic Principles of

Objectivism," was taught by Nathaniel Branden. It developed into The Nathaniel Branden Institute, which taught courses as diverse as the application of Objectivism to psychology, economics, and esthetics. Ayn Rand's ideas were marketable in and of themselves. And marketing them is what her nonfiction books do.

Rand published seven books of nonfiction. They were: *For the New Intellectual* (1961); *The Virtue of Selfishness* (1964); *Capitalism: The Unknown Ideal* (1966); *The Romantic Manifesto* (1969); *The New Left: The Anti-Industrial Revolution* (1971); *Introduction to Objectivist Epistemology* (1979); and *Philosophy: Who Needs It?* (1982). Not one of her nonfiction books is composed of predominantly original text. They are largely compilations of materials that were published previously, either in the fiction or in the various Objectivist publications. Some of the pieces are reproductions of speeches that Rand delivered in such diverse fora as West Point graduation exercises or the Ford Hall Forum.

The main sources for her nonfiction books were her periodical newsletters or journals. These publications provided a far-reaching and effective method of disseminating not only the tenets of Objectivist philosophy, but also information about activities of interest to the growing number of adherents to and students of Rand's ideas. Through the newsletters both Rand and Branden could reach a larger audience than they could in the classroom setting. On January 1, 1962, with Barbara Branden as managing editor, they undertook the publication of *The Objectivist Newsletter*, which was dedicated to explaining the application of Objectivism to contemporary problems. A fuller discussion of these newsletters follows in the summary section of this chapter. Increased circulation caused the *Newsletter* to be enlarged and presented in a magazine format which was called simply *The Objectivist*. It began publication in January of 1966. In 1971 the monthly magazine was replaced by a less formal newsletter, which Rand described as "a personal communication." *The Ayn Rand Letter* was issued fortnightly in response to the need for a wider arena. It is in these various periodicals that Rand first published the essays and treatises that were later anthologized and collected into suitable groupings for the books.

What follows are summary discussions of the major nonfiction publications. Each book will be discussed individually, but the periodicals will be discussed in three groups according to title. Summarizing anthologies is difficult. One must either summarize each of the component essays or opt for generalizations about the overall impact of the book. I have chosen the latter approach. In some cases I have cited certain specific essays for their ability to communicate the sense of the anthology. Different readers may find other emphases more to their liking. Rand's nonfiction works address complex and difficult issues and Rand's methodology is to dig for the roots of the problem and then ascend point by point to her conclusion. Therefore, it is imperative, if the reader is to understand the reasoning behind Rand's philosophical premises, that he or she read the original essays. The purpose of these summaries is to give those who have not read the works some idea of what may be found in them.

For the New Intellectual (1961)

Subtitled *The Philosophy of Ayn Rand*, this book was originally published by Random House, first in hardcover and then in paperback. For those who are interested in a capsulized version of the major themes of her fiction, this is a good place to start. The book is a compilation of excerpts from her four novels. Each excerpt is prefaced by a note in which Rand explains the context of the particular speech. As her novels became progressively more overtly didactic as well as lengthy, there are many more pages of speeches from *Atlas Shrugged* than from the other three novels combined. Eight major speeches from that novel are included; three from *The Fountainhead*; one each from *We the Living* and *Anthem*. It is in this book that Rand first publicly names her philosophy Objectivism.

The major attraction for those who have already read the novels, besides the pleasure of having all the major themes supplied in one volume, is the introductory essay in which Rand explains the background that underlies the necessity for a new group of intellectuals. Her major premises are that the historical culprits—spiritual in the forms of the church or other institutions of faith and physical in the forms of chiefs, kings, or governments—have combined to undermine the progress of individuals toward personal happiness. She calls these two forces The Witch Doctor and Attila. The third force is personified in The Producer or the reasoning person, the thinker. It is the third which is representative of the best in humanity; producers, thinkers, reasoners are people who utilize those attributes which make human survival possible.

In Rand's reading of the history of Western civilization, there are two golden periods. The first was during Aristotle's introduction of a philosophy which identified an objective reality. She credits Aristotle with liberating reason, and it was the rediscovery of his works which initiated the Renaissance, according to Rand. The second golden age was introduced by America's Founding Fathers, who established in the United States the first society in history which was created by and dominated by men of the mind, thinkers who were men of both word and deed. They inaugurated the economically free nineteenth century which Rand describes as being the period closest to laissez-faire capitalism that the world has ever achieved. In a capitalistic society the key figures are the intellectual and the businessman. Rand sees businessmen as great liberators who, through their efforts, freed the masses from eighteen-hour work days and raised the standard of living by making the latest scientific and technological discoveries popularly available. The cause of many of our current problems is that businessmen have accepted unearned guilt promulgated by intellectual altruists.

Rand indicts philosophers who have veered from Aristotelian episte- mology; she begins with Descartes and progresses chronogically through Hume, Kant (the arch-villain), Hegel, Comte, Marx, and Nietzsche. According to Rand, philosophy has brought us to this miserable state of confusion and ambiguity and therefore it is the job of philosophy to lead us out. Each person's philosophy, either explicitly or implicitly, under- girds his or her actions. All who would be intellectuals need to under- stand their philosophical premises and the implications of those prem- ises.

The Virtue of Selfishness (1964)

Rand's clarification of the essential definition of selfishness introduces this series of essays, fourteen by Rand and five by Nathaniel Branden. All except the first were originally published in The Objectivist Newslet- ter. "The Objectivist Ethics" is the reproduction of a speech delivered to a University of Wisconsin symposium. The various essays are partic- ularly helpful to a student of Objectivism or interested reader because they clarify, from a variety of perspectives, basic standards and values of Objectivism.

The introductory essay outlines the rationale of Rand's ethics. She ex- plains that life is the standard by which good is judged, therefore one's own life should be one's ethical purpose. Values are then chosen to achieve that purpose. Rand identifies Reason, Purpose, and Self-Esteem as the cardinal values of Objectivist ethics; in order to achieve those val- ues, one acts on the virtues which correspond to those values. They are: Rationality, Productiveness, and Pride. Rationality incorporates such virtues as Independence, Integrity, Honesty and Justice, all part of not faking reality. For Rand, maintenance of life and the pursuit of happi- ness are but two parts of the same whole.

A number of these essays are couched as responses to pervading bro- mides of contemporary society such as: "Who am I to judge?" or "There is no black or white, only gray," or "All life is compromise." Rand re- buts these ideas in "How Does One Lead a Rational Life in an Irra- tional Society?" "The Cult of Moral Grayness," and "Doesn't Life Re- quire Compromise?" She challenges the morality and the logic of such popular platitudes and explains why the acceptance of them is detrimen- tal to one's moral health.

Nathaniel Branden's essays on the psychological aspects of Objectivism augment Rand's philosophical perspective. In one of his sections, Branden responds to the popular argument that everyone is basically selfish, so there is no need for a philosophy which encourages selfishness. He also explains in "The Psychology of Pleasure" that the people and things that give one pleasure are a sure indication of one's values. In his discussion of romantic love and its sexual celebration, he sets the stage for ideas he was to develop, among other places, in his book *The Psychology of Romantic Love.*

The composition of this book is eclectic. Rand deals with subjects as far afield as "Racism" and "Government Financing in a Free Society." Branden discusses "Counterfeit Individualism" and "The Divine Right of Stagnation." Montaigne defined the essay as "an attempt," a brief discussion as opposed to a thesis or dissertation. These essays are just that, compressed discussions, forays into their subjects. As such they are appealing to interested nonacademic or nonspecialist readers as well as to the more serious student of Objectivism. *The Virtue of Selfishness* has been one of Rand's best-selling nonfiction works.

Capitalism: The Unknown Ideal (1966)

In this, the third of Rand's nonfiction books, the first section of theoretical and historical essays includes three articles by Alan Greenspan, one by Robert Hessen, and one by Nathaniel Branden. In the section on the current state of the nation, all the articles except "Alienation," by Nathaniel Branden, are by Rand. Rand calls the book "a collection of essays on the *moral* aspects of capitalism." Since a system of ethics must underlie any political system, Rand also reprints in this book two essays, one on rights and one on the nature of government, which were also published in *The Virtue of Selfishness.*

Rand sees capitalism as the only moral politico-economic system in history, a system which has been a great boon to humankind. Her contention is that it is being destroyed because its tenets are not being properly identified even by its loudest adherents (she calls the *Encyclopaedia Britannica* article about "Capitalism" a disgrace). Her purpose is to clearly identify the benefits of capitalism while also exposing the nature of its arch-enemy, altruism.

War, the gold standard, the airwaves, and the student rebellion are among the diverse subjects discussed in the various essays. Rand sees any initiation of force as wrong, and therefore concludes that the only moral war is a war of self-defense. She contends that capitalism inaugurated the longest period of peace in Western history: that period between the end of the Napoleonic wars in 1815 and World War I in 1914. Since she sees war as essentially looting, and since societies where there is freedom to produce do not need to loot from others, Rand concludes that capitalistic systems do not cause wars. It was the statist governments that caused World Wars I and II. Rand also thinks that the draft is an infringement on individual rights. In her view the only good army is a volunteer army and that is what results when a country is under attack as we were in World War II.

The Romantic Manifesto (1969)

Much of the appeal of Objectivism is that it is inclusive. Given the basic values and attitudes, one can then form opinions about every subject from abortion to literary criticism. Moving from her definition of art as "a selective re-creation of reality according to an artist's metaphysical value-judgments," Rand then proceeds to show the connections between art and a sense of life, explain the basic principles of literature, define Romanticism, and articulate the goals of her writing. Rand identifies herself as a writer of Romantic realism and damns the abandonment of rational esthetics as the cause of the contemporary degradation of art.

The Romantic Manifesto is perhaps the most unified and coherent of Rand's nonfiction works. Rand explains the importance of art to human consciousness. Art concretizes abstractions and thereby provides images that integrate an incalculable number of concepts. Rand's philosophy of literature develops from an Aristotelian base. Aristotle justified the importance of literature by explaining that history represents things only as they are, whereas poetry (literature) represents them as they might be or ought to be. As a medium for communicating a moral ideal, art is indispensable. And communicating moral ideals in the persons of her heroes and heroines is exactly what Rand's art does. If she were to write a dedication page for an anthology of all her works, it would read "To the glory of man," Rand explains.

Rand sees nineteenth-century Romanticism as a product of an Aristotelian sense of life, sans the undergirding philosophy, fueled by capitalism and rebellion against the prevailing Classicist establishment. Ironically, it was the Classicists who were seen as the exemplars of reason and the Romantics as advocates of the *primacy of emotions*; Rand calls this "definition by non-essentials" and explains that it is the *primacy of values* that distinguished the Romantics. By Rand's definition the greatest purely Romantic novelists are Victor Hugo and Feodor Dostoevsky; the greatest playwrights, Friedrich Schiller and Edmond Rostand. Novels that she cites for their Romantic vision are *Quo Vadis* and *The Scarlet Letter*. Among second-ranked Romanticists she names Walter Scott and Alexander Dumas. O. Henry, for his zestfully childlike and ever inventive imagination, is her candidate for the greatest popularizer of Romanticism's psychological mission of making life interesting.

Naturalism is the antithesis of Romanticism. Whereas Romanticism proceeds from a moral base and the concept of human beings as capable of free will, Naturalism attempts a non-judgmental approach and depicts humans as the victims of a deterministic universe. Rand points out the flaws in this deterministic view. Shakespeare is seen as the spiritual father of nineteenth-century Naturalism and Honoré Balzac and Leo Tolstoy as his heirs. All maintained an abstract level of characterization, presenting their views on a metaphysical level. Rand admires them more than those who succumbed to Emile Zola's journalistic methods. The title of "the most evil book in serious literature," however, is reserved for *Anna Karenina* which Rand says carries an anti-happiness message. Though she does not agree with their literary philosophy, she cites Sinclair Lewis and John O'Hara as the best representatives of contemporary Naturalism.

A special bonus at the end of the book is Rand's short story, "The Simplest Thing in the World." Written in 1940 and originally published in *The Objectivist*, it is the story of artistic integrity. While his mind naturally invents challenging, iconoclastic plots and characters, Henry Dorn tries to convince himself that "the simplest thing in the world" would be to compromise and give the public the old clichés it seems to want. However, for an artist, that proves too difficult. The story has a strong autobiographical strain as the critics misunderstand Henry Dorn's work in much the same way early critics missed the point in Rand's work. Dorn is also counseled, as Rand was, to be practical, to write what the public wants. He cannot, as Rand could not, which leaves him in an unresolved situation at the end of the story. Fortunately for us, Rand's story ended in triumph for herself and the public. The times proved that there is a large body of the public that wants to be challenged, that is hungry for ideals.

The New Left: The Anti-Industrial Revolution (1971)

Published in 1971, during the thick of that period called the "sixties," but, which in fact, lasted till the mid-seventies, this book's attacks on hippies and "smorgasbord education" may seem dated. However, as Rand's predictions about the negative results of some of the practices she rails against come about, one begins to appreciate the perceptiveness of her critique. The specific audience for this book is college students and those who are concerned about them and about modern education. Compiled and published in paperback at the suggestion of a graduate student, the work is seen by Rand as providing intellectual ammunition for students who seek a rational explanation for the activities of the New Left and the campus chaos left in their wake. The first essay, "Cashing-In: The Student 'Rebellion,' " was initially published in *The Objectivist Newsletter* and then in *Capitalism: The Unknown Ideal*. The rest of the articles were originally published in *The Objectivist* except for one that was written for the *New York Times Magazine*.

The most comprehensive of the articles included in this book is "The Comprachicos," a five-part chronicle of the destructive effects of American education. Rand begins with a translation from Victor Hugo's *The Man Who Laughs* which describes a seventeenth-century association, the *comprachicos* (children buyers), which purposefully deformed children in order to create freaks that would be saleable as entertainment for courts and sideshows. She then develops the thesis that our progressive nursery schools begin an educational process that stunts the mind in a manner analogous to the way the comprachicos twisted the bodies of the hapless children that fell into their clutches. For Rand the horror is compounded because "the comprachicos of the mind" do their mutilations openly. John Dewey takes his licks in this indictment of the American educational system, as do the "look-see" technique of teaching reading that replaced phonetics, and the discussion method of classroom teaching. "The Comprachicos" is a good illustration of Rand's predictive abilities. Her sweeping indictment of American education was called reactionary in its time, but today her criticisms are in keeping with the conclusions of the President's Commission on Education.

In "The Anti-Industrial Revolution" Rand's analysis of the failure of old-line Marxism and the consequent support that new-line leftists give to anti-industrial and ecological movements provides food for thought. Since the promise of socialist abundance has not become a reality in Soviet Russia, Socialist Britain, or other European Communist countries, the new-line attack indicts capitalism for creating its abundance by denuding the landscape and polluting the environment. Of course, many of the antinuclear, anti-industrial, and ecological movements' adherents are not leftists, but Rand's inferences about their utilization by anticapitalist propagandists are still valid.

Foretelling the bankruptcy of collectivist welfare states is another example of Rand's perceptiveness. It is not surprising that Margaret Thatcher, who has turned around some of the negative effects of Britain's socialist policies, is an admirer of the writings of Ayn Rand. Rand's arguments for the life-expanding aspects of industrialization remind us, lest we become too enamored of an idyllic representation of the pastoral past, of the many ways our lives have been benefited by the technological advances that we take for granted.

Introduction to Objectivist Epistemology (1979)

A theory of knowledge is basic to philosophy, and as all knowledge is acquired and stored in conceptual form, Rand chooses to introduce her theories on epistemology by presenting her theory of concepts. Before we can determine what we know, we must determine how concepts are formed, what their nature is, how we can assure their validity.

Though it was published in 1979, this book is composed wholly of materials originally published over a decade earlier in *The Objectivist*. Rand's essay was also issued as a separate monograph by the Objectivist Book Service. In addition to Rand's eight-part essay, Leonard Peikoff's article, "The Analytic-Synthetic Dichotomy," which was also originally published in *The Objectivist*, is included.

Rand begins with the axiom: "Existence exists." By accepting the axiom, one acknowledges that something exists which one can perceive and that one has a tool by which to perceive it (consciousness). "Existence exists" means that there is a reality independent of anyone's ability to perceive it. Rand moves from the essential axiom to an explication of how one develops knowledge about that reality through sensations, percepts, and concepts. The importance of the mathematical process of measurement to the formation of concepts is explained, as are the processes of concept formation and the development of abstractions.

Special kinds of concepts such as concepts of consciousness and axiomatic concepts are also discussed. Rand explains that consciousness is experienced in relation to an external world. To be aware—to be conscious—is to be conscious of something. Consciousness has two attributes: content and action. Rand discusses the interrelationship of those two attributes at some length, distinguishing among concepts of cognition, concepts of method, and concepts of evaluation. Rand defines axiomatic concepts as those which identify a primary fact of reality, i.e., one that cannot be reduced or broken down into smaller parts. Existence, identity and consciousness are the fundamental axiomatic concepts; they cannot be proved and need no proof.

The special relationship of language to concept formation is discussed in the chapter on definitions. Rand's definition of language is "a code of visual-auditory symbols that serve the psycho-epistemological function of converting concepts into the mental equivalent of concretes." A definition, therefore, differentiates one concept from all other concepts as it identifies the distinguishing characteristics of the concept it defines. Rand credits Aristotle with being the first to formulate the principle of correct definitions; however, he believed that definitions referred to metaphysical essences. It is on the issue of essences that Objectivism differs from Aristotle. Objectivism holds that the nature of essences is epistemological, not metaphysical. Rand differentiates Objectivism from the four schools of thought on the issue of concepts because it is the only philosophy that regards concepts as *objective*, derived from reality by the human mind, not revealed or invented.

A summary is provided at the end of the eight chapters. While it is useful, the subject matter is so abstruse that unless one is well versed in epistemology, I would not recommend relying on the summary.

Peikoff's "The Analytic-Synthetic Dichotomy" is a rebuttal of the prevailing philosophical contention that analytic truths are merely definitional and that synthetic truths are contingent, uncertain, and unprovable. Objectivism, which holds that "existence is a self-sufficient primary," rejects the metaphysical arguments of much of contemporary philosophy.

Philosophy: Who Needs It? (1982)

Published posthumously, Ayn Rand's last anthology is introduced and organized by Leonard Peikoff, her literary heir. Rand was working on it when she died. There is no new material in the book; most of the essays were originally published in *The Ayn Rand Letter*. The title article was first delivered as a graduation address at West Point.

Rand's premise, that everyone's actions or inactions derive from a conscious or unconscious philosophy, is convincingly illustrated in a number of the preliminary essays. Rand uncovers the philosophical underpinnings for the beliefs and behavior of many contemporary intellectuals, as well as amoralists and those with "anti-conceptual" mentalities. She illustrates how the philosophies of Hume, Kant, Plato, James, and Emerson influence thinking even though, more often than not, the average individual is not aware of the source of such postulates as "Don't be so sure—nobody can be certain of anything," or "It may be true for you, but it is not true for me."

One of Rand's greatest gifts is her ability to cut to the heart of a contemporary event or issue and analyze its philosophical implications. The essay "Kant versus Sullivan" is one example of Rand operating with that kind of critical clarity. Using the broadway play, *The Miracle Worker*, which is based on the true life account of how Anne Sullivan brought Helen Keller, who was both deaf and blind, into the realm of conceptual awareness, Rand cogently illustrates the undeniable significance of *the word*, of language. It is through the word that Helen is able to break out of her limited world of sensations and become a communicating part of the human family. Given that importance, Rand then castigates those academicians who publish articles that devalue the word and postulate "science without experience," and language without words.

The Objectivist Newsletter (January 1962–December 1965)

Edited and published by Ayn Rand and Nathaniel Branden, with Barbara Branden as managing editor and Elayne Kalberman as circulation manager, *The Objectivist Newsletter* includes articles and reviews by Barbara Branden, Alan Greenspan, Leonard Peikoff, Edith Efron, and Robert Hessen. Beatrice Hessen, Joan Blumenthal, Martin Anderson, and Joan Meltzer each contribute one review. The core of the newsletter, however, is provided by Rand and Branden. Most issues contain major commentary by each. The newsletter format provided for a front-page editorial essay which dealt with some aspect of contemporary culture, politics, or ethics; the "Intellectual Ammunition Department" answered questions by readers in order to help them respond effectively to political and philosophical challenges to Objectivism. The "Books" section generally reviewed works of philosophy, history, and economics. (See the Appendix for a list of books favorably reviewed in Objectivist publications). Occasionally a second article, either by a guest columnist or by either one of the editors who did not write the front page essay, amplified the issue. The "Objectivist Calendar" provided information about publications, classes, lectures, readings, art shows and even social events sponsored by the Nathaniel Branden Institute. The tone of these newsletters is exhilarating and self-confident. They exude a sense of accomplishment and excitement which is best exemplified in Nathaniel Branden's yearly "A Report to Our Readers," wherein the continuing progress of Objectivism is reviewed. In the December 1965 issue he is able to announce the transition from the newsletter to a magazine format for *The Objectivist*.

Rand and Branden cover a variety of subjects in their articles and "intellectual ammunition" responses. The first article in the first issue echoes a theme from *Atlas Shrugged*, "Check Your Premises." In it Rand warns all advocates of freedom about internal enemies that are more dangerous to our individual liberties than the threats from Russia or any other foreign country. The two culprits she names are the Federal Communications Commission and antitrust laws. She denounces contemporary conservatives for having lost their philosophical base, thus becoming reactors rather than actors. Rand points out that politics is but a branch of philosophy and that a consistent political theory is necessarily based on supporting metaphysics, epistemology, and ethics. Because of their basic philosophy, Objectivists are "radicals for capitalism," not conservatives.

Subsequent issues take up the questions of the FCC and antitrust laws. Rand calls antitrust "The Rule of Unreason." She points out the basic contradiction of "free competition" *enforced* by law. Antitrust laws function like Catch–22; businessmen can be prosecuted for prices that are too high, too low, or regulated. Since business people are the one group that distinguishes capitalism from totalitarian governments, their position being usurped by bureaucrats and commissars in collectivist states, then if we value our freedom, we should fight for the rights of business people. In her denunciation of Newton N. Minow, then chairman of the FCC, Rand explains the contradiction of allowing one man to decide what is in "the public interest." Minow had announced that any television or radio station that did not meet his criterion of public service would lose its license. The public expresses its interest by watching or listening to certain programs. If one person can decide that the public is not fit to judge its own interest, then cannot one person also decide that the public is not competent to decide elections, or what it should buy? Those who would protect us for our own good remove the basic freedom of choice. Rand then calls out for protection from our protectors, specifically big government which, as it creates more and more bureaus and commissions to oversee our safety, plunges us deeper and deeper into debt, creates inflation, and interferes with our individual rights. Everyone is entitled to the same protection as consumers, Rand explains; therefore, if there are regulations protecting consumers from dishonesty on the part of manufacturers, shouldn't politicians also be enjoined from marketing ideas that are hazardous to our health or life, from making misleading or mislabeled promises, from presenting a variety of programs whose hidden costs amount to a violation of truth in packaging?

The specific referents of these newsletters were events of the early sixties. What makes them intellectually satisfying today is that the basic premises Rand uses to criticize government, education, or literature apply now as they did then. When in "The Pull Peddlers" she decries the grotesquery of our citizens' lobbying for special funds and favors for foreign governments, she could not have foretold the ultimate grotesquery of the brother of a president registering as the foreign agent of a country whose leader consistently denounces the United States (Billy Carter was a registered agent for the Libyan government). Such an episode would have been called exaggerated in *Atlas Shrugged*, but as Rand was to exclaim on another occasion, she had thought she was a Romantic writer; however, current events were proving her a Naturalist.

The Objectivist (January 1966–September 1971)

Begun by Nathaniel Branden and Ayn Rand, with basically the same staff as *The Objectivist Newsletter*, *The Objectivist* is essentially the same matter but different form. The May 1968 issue publishes Rand's explanation for the dissolution of all personal and professional relationship with both Nathaniel and Barbara Branden. Subsequent issues are edited by Rand with Leonard Peikoff as associate editor.

In June and July of 1968 Rand prints "A Statement of Policy" which is her revision and redefinition of an earlier policy vis-à-vis students and supporters. Rand defines Objectivism as an intellectual movement with herself as its theoretician. Students and supporters are encouraged to study, discuss and disseminate Objectivist ideas providing they don't attempt to act as "spokesmen for Objectivism." One of Rand's main concerns was with unanointed theoreticians who appropriated and then modified and otherwise twisted her philosophy. She delineates the only authentic sources: her own works; articles appearing in *The Objectivist* and *The Objectivist Newsletter*; books by authors endorsed by the Objectivist publications; *Who Is Ayn Rand?* and articles written by Nathaniel and Barbara Branden up to that time, but not in the future.

The Ayn Rand Letter (October 1971–February 1976)

Published in a simple, typewritten letter format consisting of a fortnightly article by Rand, which was occasionally replaced with a piece by Leonard Peikoff, *The Ayn Rand Letter*'s only other feature is the "Objectivist Calendar."

There is abundant food for thought in the five years' worth of responses to national and international events. As always, Rand analyzes by boring to the underlying malignancy which causes the various symptoms she surveys. Whether it is a discussion of the disintegration of language or wage-price controls, she explains that the philosophy providing the underpinning for the majority of destructive contemporary activities is altruism, the moral base for collectivism. She also explains how irrationalism works as the epistemological base for both altruism and collectivism. Temporal events are predictable from the prevailing collectivist principles, and as Rand expounds over and over again, the battlefield must be philosophical. If one does not question the basic premises behind the issues, one cannot effectively fight them.

For those interested in presidential campaigns, there are a number of articles leading up to the Nixon-McGovern contest. Rand saw the Democratic National Convention of 1972 as the culmination of the collectivist tack the party had been taking for forty years. Especially abhorrent to her was the platform promise to "make economic security a matter of right." In order to do that, Rand explains, those who produce must be enslaved to those who don't, and it is the worst kind of logical fallacy to base one person's rights on the destruction of another's. Another of McGovern's concepts that Rand deplores is his desire to effect a "redistribution of wealth." Such a plan is based on the premise that the wealth is his, or the government's, to distribute. Rand asks the relevant question, which is: by what right would McGovern do so? A system where the government has such rights is communism. McGovern thought to use the income tax for such a purpose, but as Rand points out, this puts the burden on the productive who work. The beneficiaries of such a system are the rich who don't have to work and the nonproductive. Again, it is a matter of punishing the able for being able.

Among other issues that raise Rand's ire are (1) government grants which have the effect of forcing citizens to support ideas they are vehemently opposed to and (2) B. F. Skinner's theories, which she sees as eliminating the dignity of achievement by ascribing the differences in people to the type of reinforcement they received. One of the dangers of government grants is that when a government intrudes into the world of ideas in the form of subsidies, the result can be a set of official ideas. As grants are given to "prestigious" researchers, this is a way of keeping those who are already part of the establishment in power. As for Skinner, his utopian commune, Twin Oaks, which can't subsist on its own, is supported by government money. In a two-part article Rand repudiates Skinner's arguments along with the American Philosophical Association for celebrating him, and even the critics who gave his book *Beyond Freedom and Dignity* negative reviews for the wrong reasons.

Of particular interest to those who agree with much of what Rand has to say, but don't know how to help propagate her theories, is her 1972 response to the question "What Can One Do?" Her answer is that since the battle is philosophical, an intellectual battle is necessary. Minds must be convinced. Beginning with the self and not expecting to influence too large a group are two starting instructions. It is important to develop one's own consistent philosophy so that one can deal with challenges and questions. Rand cautions against joining the wrong ideological groups because they seem to espouse views with which one agrees while their fundamental principles conflict with much that one believes in. Examples she gives are the Libertarians, and conservative parties. Ad hoc committees she finds acceptable because they usually have but one goal. Above all, Rand counsels people to speak out. Speak out against the irrational. Do not keep silent.

In November of 1975 Ayn Rand announced that she would have to cease publication of *The Ayn Rand Letter*. The *Letter* had fallen way behind schedule. The August 1974 issue had been written in May of 1975, at which time Rand announced that she would change the fortnightly schedule to a monthly format. However, even that was too burdensome. In "A Last Survey" she carefully and explicitly outlines her reasons for her readers. The wonder is not that at the age of seventy she was quitting an onerous schedule of bimonthly or monthly philosophical articles along with all the other obligations she faced; the wonder is that for fourteen years she was able to supply the various newsletters with a steady stream of philosophical responses to events of the times.

CHAPTER 5

Criticism of Rand's Works

Rand is a polemical writer and therefore it is not surprising that she arouses heated reaction from a variety of sources. There are some who vilify her; the adjective "fascist" comes easily to the tongues of those on the left. There are others who idolize her; she had many disciples in her lifetime and students of Objectivism have been curiously blind to any imperfections in the articulator of the philosophy. Blind adoration and faith in Rand's precepts are so often characteristic of her followers that the word "cult" has been applied to Rand's adherents. One of the critical works that will be discussed in this chapter asks the pointed question: "Is Objectivism a Religion?" Politically, Rand is an anomaly; she antagonizes liberals and conservatives equally.

The purpose of this chapter is to synopsize the critical reaction to Rand so that readers of her works can evaluate both the thoughtful and the vituperative. I have included major commentary from both scholarly and popular publications. However, interest in Rand does not confine itself to expression in either the mass media or academic journals. Much interest in her is expressed in sources that are not routinely indexed. A character drawn from her theories is the hero of an arcane comic book;[1] a contemporary rock group dedicated an album to her spirit.[2]

Rand's arguments are persuasive. The pictures she creates of the ills and monsters of contemporary society appeal to our frustrations with a government which has mushroomed out of control and personal vistas that seem increasingly circumscribed. The strength of her arguments and the simplicity of her solutions are convincing reasons to accept her explanations for what has gone awry and her prescriptions for treating a variety of contemporary maladies. But, as one of Rand's major messages is that one must use independent judgment, it is important to weigh and evaluate refutation and analysis of her theories also.

Part Two and Part Three of the Bibliography contain a listing of all the books, articles, and reviews of Rand's works as well as the references to her which were read by this author in the preparation of *The Ayn Rand Companion*. This chapter serves to annotate many of those items. Book-length studies will be summarized individually; representative articles and reviews are treated in the bibliographical essays that follow the book summaries. The purpose of the bibliographical essays is to give a sense of the kinds of criticism and reviews Rand's works elicited; therefore only certain illustrative pieces are mentioned individually. The essays are in no way meant to be comprehensive. Though I would expect all readers will want to make their own evaluations of the efficacy of the criticism, I have pointed out some of the more obvious critical biases and inconsistencies. The books are arranged chronologically.

BOOKS

Who Is Ayn Rand? (1962)
by Nathaniel Branden and Barbara Branden

The first full-length work to be published about Ayn Rand was written by her disciples and partners in the dissemination of Objectivist philosophy. For nearly a generation, that nineteen-year period in which Rand's literary star blazed brightest, the Brandens were her closest associates. *Who Is Ayn Rand?* both benefits and suffers from that close perspective. On the plus side, Barbara Branden's biographical essay, a response to the title question, provides the only detailed memoir of the life of a woman who was very secretive about her private life and history. Even Rand's full real name was not known to the Brandens until Ms. Branden unearthed it in the recent research for her forthcoming biography.

Nathaniel Branden's essays about Rand's literary methodology and the implications of her philosophy for psychology, and a detailed analysis of "The Moral Revolution in *Atlas Shrugged*," are synoptic and illuminating. As an authorized vita, however, *Who Is Ayn Rand?* is guilty of the limitations of that genre: only that which Rand approved is included. Nathaniel Branden has repudiated the book publicly and in print. In 1971 he expressed the wish that the book had never been written. "If it were possible to prevent its further distribution, I would do so," he said in an interview with *Reason* magazine.[3]

Barbara Branden has also stated that though the material presented in her biographical essay was written in good faith, the portrait of Rand that it develops is one-sided and does not represent the total picture.[4]

Is Objectivism a Religion? (1968)
by Albert Ellis, Ph.D.

Ellis readily identifies himself as an opponent of Objectivism. In fact, this book resulted from his inability to complete his "objections to Ob-

jectivism" within the time frame and strictures of a public debate between himself and Nathaniel Branden. Ellis not only finds fault with
Objectivism's claim to rationality, but he also indicts it as detrimental
to the psychological well-being of its practitioners. Ellis' main thesis is
that Objectivism, for all its claims of rationality, is a religion; his methodology is to enumerate the ten characteristics of "true believers" and
then to illustrate how Objectivists exemplify those qualities to a lesser or
greater degree.

Like most critics, Ellis is best at fault-finding. His arguments also suf-
fer from an obvious self-serving bias: he is promoting his own rational-
emotive psychotherapy. Another deficiency in Ellis' criticism is his lack
of standards. While Rand and Branden work from a value hierarchy,
Ellis refuses to judge. In his system, even the individual who is "wrong,
mistaken, and irresponsible," and who *chooses* to commit wrong deeds,
need not be condemned. Curiously, however, while Ellis is careful not
to convict wrongdoers, he is quick to condemn Rand.

His techniques, too often, are name-calling and circular argument.
His response to Rand's claim that the best product at the cheapest price
would win in the marketplace is, "This is arrant hogwash, as virtually
any reasonably intelligent high school student of economics should be
able to see."[5] While this kind of posturing is dramatic, it rests on a logical fallacy. To Ellis' credit, he does explain how Rand's statement does
not take into account vagaries of the marketplace, such as fads, and consumers who might not be rational.

"Sheer drivel," he exclaims on one page; "Balderdash," he cries on
the next. Although such opening ripostes as "What claptrap!" tend to
detract from the serious character of his criticism, he does follow such
flippancies with some salient observations about aspects of capitalism and
human nature that Rand ignores.

The most telling argument for the aptness of Ellis' criticisms came
shortly after his book was published. Following his "excommunication,"
Nathaniel Branden made statements that corroborate the validity of some
of Ellis' arguments. In an interview with *Reason* magazine Branden explains that his book *The Disowned Self* is, among other things, an attempt to undo the damage he had done to students of Objectivism by
inadvertently encouraging them to distrust their emotions.[6] His statement lends credence to Ellis' that Objectivism had a strong negative effect on the emotional health of its devotees. Ellis also excoriates Objectivists for being too judgmental and intolerant; rather than wanting to
understand wrongdoers, he says, they want "to ruthlessly squelch, per-
secute, annihilate them." Ellis refers to Rand's hostility and anger when
questioned in a way she did not find suitable. Branden acknowledges
that in the early days of the movement, he too had treated questioners
too harshly, but that as his attitude changed, he tried to mitigate Rand's
cruel treatment of unfortunates who antagonized her.

Much of the pleasure of reading Ellis results from the verbal high jinks of its author. It is a pleasure similar to the one derived from extravagant satire; one is amused by the exaggeration. However, occasionally the same extravagance and exaggeration detract from the serious nature of the arguments.

With Charity toward None (1971)
by William F. O'Neill

O'Neill's is the first evenhanded book dealing with Rand's philosophies. He has no axe to grind as Ellis does, nor is he a disciple as the Brandens were. His is a reasonable, detailed analysis of the validity of the basic philosophical propositions of Objectivism. O'Neill's purpose is to answer two questions: (1) Are Rand's principles rational (valid/consistent)? (2) Are they true empirically?

O'Neill's methodology is to examine Rand's precepts by as objective as possible application of the scientific verification process. Although his critique is generally negative and he finds Rand "guilty of occasional inconsistencies, contradictions and ambiguities," he also expresses admiration for Rand's intellectual and moral courage. O'Neill appreciates Rand's importance as "a useful intellectual catalyst in a society which frequently suffers from philosophical 'tired blood.' "[7]

In O'Neill's evaluation, Rand asks the right questions even if she postulates the wrong answers. He is especially approving of the fact that she has provoked so many people into thinking.

It Usually Begins with Ayn Rand (1972)
by Jerome Tuccille

Tuccille has the appealing quality of being able to laugh at himself. He also manages to poke fun at everyone else. Only the first two chapters of this book are about Rand, specifically; the rest of the book is a wild and wacky sojourn through the confusion of right-wing politics. The book is sub-titled "A Libertarian Odyssey."

Like other critics, Tuccille notes contradictions in Rand's application of her own philosophy. He is particularly devastating in his satire of Objectivist cabals in Rand's apartment. Tuccille points out the irony in the Communist-style purges of those who did not toe the Rand line, Rand being such a vehement opponent of communism. Rand negated her own principles of rationality and individualism by not allowing any deviation from her interpretation of reality. He calls Objectivism "a wonderfully appealing religion substitute."

Answer to Ayn Rand: A Critique of the Philosophy of Objectivism (1974)
by John W. Robbins

John W. Robbins does not pretend to objectivity; his stated purpose is "to correct a new and growing movement in America." He describes his thesis straightforwardly: "The argument of this book will be destructive; it will attempt to demonstrate that Objectivism is self-contradictory, that its epistemology must lead to skepticism, its metaphysics to the void, its ethics to hedonism, and its politics to anarchy."[8]

Robbins is most effective in delineating inconsistencies in Objectivism. For example, he accuses Rand of smuggling a great deal of Christianity into Objectivism. What he either fails to understand or does not know is that the ideas he accuses her of lifting existed prior to the birth and practice of Christianity. The archetype of the hero/savior leading a select and elect group to a utopia is certainly not exclusively Christian.

In the initial section of the book, Robbins unfolds a well-argued, logical critique. Finally, to the trusting reader's consternation, logic is abandoned. In the discussion of metaphysics, Robbins' frame of reference is made clear. Robbins does not believe in reason; he is a champion of revelation. His book is a response to Rand in the name of Jesus Christ. What he is doing is proselytizing for Christianity as the only basis for a free and stable society.

The Philosophical Thought of Ayn Rand (1984)
edited by Douglas J. Den Uyl and Douglas B. Rasmussen

Den Uyl and Rasmussen's book is a major contribution to Rand scholarship. Its significance is underscored by a number of factors. Not only is it the first book about Rand to be published in ten years, but it was completed after her death and therefore has the benefit of dealing with a relatively complete body of her work.

Den Uyl and Rasmussen state their intention, which is "to evaluate Rand according to the same scholarly standards that would apply to any philosopher."[9] They also seek to move the discussion of Rand out of the range of the personal and into the realm of serious scholarship. One of the ongoing complaints of Rand students and admirers has been the refusal of "intellectuals" to accord her serious attention. The fact that this book is being published by a university press should contribute to its effectiveness in initiating attention in academic circles. In order "to maintain a consistent level of professional standards" the editors have collected a group of essays by academicians who are also acknowledged thinkers in their own right.

The anthology is divided into three sections: Metaphysics, Ethics, and

Politics. Each section begins with an interpretive essay by Den Uyl and Rasmussen in which they explain Rand's basic hypotheses in those three fields. Following their introductory pieces are critical essays by Wallace Matson and Robert Hollinger in the area of metaphysics; Jack Wheeler, J. Charles King, and Eric Mack in the ethics section; and Anthony Flew and Tibor R. Machan on politics. The essays are perceptive and enlightening. They are marked by a willingness to acknowledge the validity of some of Rand's contentions while pointing out what the individual authors consider to be gaps in her knowledge and errors in her thinking. More important, they are an essential element in assuring that her ideas will be perpetuated. As Wallace Matson so tellingly explains, "intellectual progress is inextricably bound up with critical give-and-take."[10] The only alternative to critical dialogue is stagnation.

While the quality of these essays is impressive, some are more available to the lay reader than others. As all the contributors are philosophers, writing for an academic press, terminology and allusions that are commonplace for them are not readily comprehensible to those outside of the discipline. For those, however, who are serious in their desire to see Rand's philosophy subjected to critical analysis, the study is well worth the effort.

Except for *Who Is Ayn Rand?* and *The Philosophical Thought of Ayn Rand*, the books about Rand are generally the works of detractors. Only the Brandens, and then Leonard Peikoff who succeeded them as Rand's literary heir, have been close enough to this very private woman to gather sufficient first-hand material for a book about her and her theories. As Rand promulgated the theory that her thoughts were her property and threatened suit against anyone who tried to capitalize upon them, even the sympathetic have been frightened away from such projects. What has resulted is a polarization of her critics. Perhaps, now that she is dead, there will be a more receptive attitude on the part of her heir toward "unauthorized" publication projects. The only way important writers can be given their due is in the open interchange which characterizes the building of a critical reputation.

There is one book, as yet unpublished, which should hold great interest for Rand students and enthusiasts. Barbara Branden is writing an unauthorized biography, tentatively titled *The Passion of Ayn Rand*. As Ms. Branden has all the tapes from her original interviews for *Who Is Ayn Rand?* plus the benefit of a long intimacy with Rand, this biography should provide a detailed and authentic portrait of Ayn Rand as both writer and person. Ms. Branden and her research assistant, Terry Diamond, have been indefatigable in their efforts to gather information from every possible source.

ARTICLES

Most of the articles written about Ayn Rand's novels are concerned with the effects of her ideas on her readers. The strength of her appeal both amazes and frightens her detractors. In the *New York Times Book Review* silver anniversary article about *The Fountainhead*, Nora Ephron promises herself never to read the book again, although she professes to "still have a great affection for it and [would] recommend it to anyone taking a plane trip." Though deeply affected by the book when she was eighteen, Ephron calls "the most astonishing phenomenon in publishing history" a silly book and claims that the young are fascinated by *The Fountainhead* because they miss the point.[11]

After cataloging Rand's deficiencies as both writer and public persona, Barbara Grizzuti Harrison muses about the bases of Rand's attraction for so many women. Harrison's conclusion is that the appeal is largely due to the power of the fantasy of a strong, dominant woman who is overpowered by an even stronger and more dominant male who is yet willing to lay all of his power at the feet of the heroine. Harrison is appalled and theorizes that narcissism, low self-esteem, and the appeal of selfishness after a lifetime of traditionally feminine sacrificial behavior account for Rand's appeal to the female psyche. Harrison admits that Rand's appeal includes men, particularly the middle class; she accuses Rand of pandering to their fears. Harrison concludes, "I am afraid of Ayn Rand."[12]

Like Harrison, Bruce Cook is fearful of Rand's influence. Writing as both a Catholic and a liberal, Cook is seriously concerned with Rand's ability "to attract adolescents and the Far Right." He views her lack of charity and contempt for religion as damaging for her followers. More than once, he makes allusions that compare her theories to fascism.[13]

John Kobler, more bemused at Rand's appeal than concerned for the souls of her adherents, is not as condemnatory as Cook. In his "Curious Cult of Ayn Rand" he labels Rand "the Joan of Arc of Free Enterprise," while in a flip tone he suggests that her "code of ethics [is] likely to appall even the greediest dollar chaser."[14]

One of the persons most upset by Rand's influence on young people is Robert L. White, who as an English professor at the University of Kentucky in the early sixties found Rand the novelist who most impressed his students. White is appalled, not just because he finds Rand "a horrendously bad writer," but because of her ideas which he finds more horrifying than her writing. He calls her a "hipster on the right" and suggests that her revulsion against "square" society is not unlike that of the "hipster" or the "beatnik."[15] Some twenty years later Jeff Riggenbach makes a similar contention. In "The Disowned Children of Ayn

Rand" he calls not only the hippies of the 1960s but also the militant feminists, gay activists, and pursuers of self-realization in the "Me Decade" of the 1970s Randians.[16] What both White and Riggenbach contend is that young people read Rand's novels, not her philosophical works, and therefore they interpret her in terms of their own perspectives. White thinks that students who are in rebellion against their elders and in search of their own identities associate themselves with Rand's characters who are individuals who do what they think is right and damn the establishment. Riggenbach also notes that Rand's heroic characters are described in youthful images, images which appeal to those whose watchword was "don't trust anyone over thirty." Though Rand denounced the dominant student movements of the sixties, calling them "savages" and "contorted young creatures," she did so in her newsletters and nonfiction works, and there is no reason to believe that the beatniks, hippies, or other students who "dug" Rand ever read those.

Another article that contributes to the overall image of Rand as a strong influence on young people is an interview in *Mademoiselle* which makes her part of the magazine's "Disturber of the Peace" series.

While many of Rand's detractors were concerned with the potency of Rand's effects on young people in general, another target for negative criticism was the growing number of Objectivists and students of Objectivism, those people who identified themselves with or wished to be identified as followers of Rand's philosophy.[17] Prior to Ellis' *Is Objectivism a Religion?* Nora Sayre's article "The Cult of Ayn Rand" derided the zealotry of Rand's followers. Sayre calls Rand the "abbess of the acute Right" and satirizes not only Rand but also Nathaniel Branden and the audience members at NBI courses.[18] Sayre's ridicule of the level of conformity and unquestioning admiration required of Rand's followers predated Tuccille's more detailed savaging of the smaller meetings of Rand's inner circle. After his break with Rand, Nathaniel Branden, himself the object of much of the satire, joined those who condemned Rand's demands of unswerving loyalty and agreement from her followers. In "Break Free!" an interview published by *Reason* magazine, Branden acknowledges his role in perpetuating the Ayn Rand mystique and "contributing to that dreadful atmosphere of intellectual repressiveness that pervades the Objectivist movement."[19]

Following up on Sayre's description of the cultish quality of Objectivism, Dora Jane Hamblin's *Life* magazine article the following year has the same title as Sayre's with the word "angry" inserted to describe Rand. In Hamblin's view, Objectivists were humorless, "ragingly individualistic" adulators of Rand and her philosophy. Hamblin notes the irony of this anti-collectivist movement's "almost conspiratorial" communist cell-like fervor.[20]

A *Newsweek* article, which generally deprecates her novels, her philosophy, and her followers, compares Rand to Aimee McPherson as a she-messiah who can hypnotize an audience. The article concludes that Rand is "a welcome streak of color in the world of authorship"—a "born eccentric."[21]

Generally missing from the body of Rand criticism in periodicals or newspapers are articles that are the works of neither detractors nor adherents, but simply studies that either specifically or generally deal with Rand's works or ideas in and of themselves. There are few essays that do not approach Rand's work from a biographical perspective. Rand not only as author but as public personality looms large over most of the pieces written about her in the 1960s and 1970s.

Rand's works are treated with more equanimity in professional journals. Though her literary works have been generally ignored by academic critics, there are a few articles about her novels that discuss Rand's books from a pedagogical perspective. In 1966 *Anthem* was included in a *New York Times Book Review* article about the favorite books of high-school students. With *Anthem* obviously still a favorite in 1983, the article "*Anthem*: A Book for All Reasons" suggests sixteen student projects for either high-school or junior college readers of *Anthem* and recommends the book as one that lends itself well to the discussion of the shaping devices of fiction, i.e., symbols, irony, and mythology, and one that holds the reader's interest.[22] My own study in *College English*, "Ayn Rand and Feminism: An Unlikely Alliance" recommends *Atlas Shrugged* for women's studies courses because of its portrayal of an adult, self-actualized, and able heroine and a number of its themes which reinforce feminist premises.[23]

"Ayn Rand's Neurotic Personalities of Our Times" is one of the few articles that deals seriously with Rand as a novelist. Paul Deane not only finds the characters in *The Fountainhead* "thoroughly realized" and motivated in a "psychologically valid" manner, but he points out close resemblances between Rand's characters and certain personality types identified by Karen Horney in *The Neurotic Personality of Our Time* (1937).[24] Philip Gordon's "The Extroflective Hero: A Look at Ayn Rand" uses F. S. Perls' *Ego, Hunger and Aggression* as the basis for a generally negative analysis of the egoism of Rand's heroes.[25]

In "Ayn Rand's Promethean Heroes" John Cody notes the long overdue need to subject Rand's novels to "objective and persuasive literary analysis." Cody's contribution is to trace Rand's self-conscious use of a Promethean sense of life, a vision that proclaims the value of an heroic self-assertion against the established order. Iris Murdoch and Ayn Rand are compared and contrasted in "The Girder and the Trellis" by Kathleen Collins. The problem with the last two articles is that though they bemoan the lack of critical attention to Rand in the established organs of academic criticism, they are published not in scholarly journals but in *Reason* magazine, a Libertarian publication.[26]

While attention to Rand's literary works is still scant, she has received some serious notice in social science journals, and as the zeitgeist becomes increasingly less hospitable to leftist liberalism, she will probably inspire more consideration. Her anti-collectivism and moral defense of capitalism have influenced a number of important politicians outside of our country. Besides the more well-known leaders Margaret Thatcher and Malcolm Fraser, there was Anders Lange, who headed a Norwegian Party for the Reduction of Taxes and Other Duties and Government Interference.

An important study in the *British Journal of Political Science*, in its review of what is called "The New Liberalism," divides Libertarians or "new liberals" or the radical right into two main groups: the "consequentialists" and the "rights theorists." Ayn Rand and Robert Nozick are singled out as the most important "rights theorists." Murray N. Rothbard's theories are seen as a combination of the two groups. Not only are Rand's argument for egoism as a moral doctrine of capitalism and her rejection of altruism valued as original contributions to "rights" theories, but her ideas are seen as catalysts for further innovation in Libertarian thinking, i.e., in the works of Tibor Machan and Eric Mack.[27]

Rand's works are regularly mentioned in both the texts and bibliographies of a number of recent articles having to do with individual rights, the sociology of thought, and psychology. In these articles Rand is cited both for her influence on a number of contemporary theorists and as a purveyor of a significant ideology. (See Part III of the Bibliography.)

Books and articles about Rand's works of philosophy far exceed those about her novels. Many of the articles about Rand's philosophy appeared in the philosophical journal *Personalist* in the 1970s. In one intellectual interchange Robert Nozick's rendition of Rand's argument for property is challenged by Tibor Machan and then by Douglas Den Uyl and Douglas Rasmussen.[28] Machan claims that Nozick paraphrases Rand inaccurately and that actually Nozick and Rand hold the same view.[29] Den Uyl and Rasmussen also argue that Nozick misstates and misunderstands Rand's position; they offer their own interpretation.[30] Rand's position on property rights is also challenged by George T. Mavrodes, who thinks the notion of property rights should be abandoned for the notion of a divisible set of rights.[31]

Rand's choice of a name for her philosophy and the consistency and integrity of her theories were questioned by a number of writers. Stephen E. Taylor asks the question, "Is Ayn Rand Really Selfish, or Only Confused?"[32] He finds her moral philosophy inconsistent and its basic tenets unsubstantiated. Kenneth J. Smith analyzes the similarities between Rand's ideas and the principal hypotheses of Existentialism.[33] Prior to Smith's juxtaposing of Objectivism and Existentialism, Hazel Barnes devoted a chapter of her book *An Existentialist Ethics* to Rand's philosophy which she terms "Egoistic Humanism."[34] Acknowledging Rand's expressed contempt for Existentialism, Barnes still sees much in common between the Rand hero and the Existentialist: "both Objectivism and Existentialism call for the assertion of the free individual against those theologies and those oppressively conformist societies which seek to make him deny his unique self in the interests of ready-made social molds and values."[35] Then Barnes analyzes those areas in which Rand and Sartre agree and those in which they part company. Using Rand's article "Racism" as an example, Barnes points out Rand's questionable reading of history, loose application of terminology, and naive confidence; Rand's attitude toward the Negroes' civil rights demands is also seen as an example of her sacrificing certain lesser principles to her most basic principle: "that the government must never interfere with the self-interest of employers or property owners."[36] Barnes finds the dollar sign as unsatisfactory as the cross as a symbol for human aspirations.

Tibor Machan is among the philosophers who have written most consistently and most positively about Rand. In his editorial introduction to the special Ayn Rand Issue of *Reason*, Machan takes exception to those who insult Rand because they disagree with her. While he also disagrees with her on some particulars, Machan believes that Rand is "one of the great geniuses of our time," though he is not sure she has spent enough time working out crucial areas of her philosophy to insure her place in the history of philosophy. Machan concludes that she may be remembered as much for her influence on others as for her original works.[37] In "Ayn Rand: A Contemporary Heretic?" Machan outlines Rand's heretical positions in five areas of philosophy: metaphysics, ethics, epistemology, politics, and aesthetics.[38]

Roy A. Childs, Jr., is another writer who, though he may disagree with Rand in certain areas, has written positively about her. "An Open Letter to Ayn Rand: Objectivism and the State" is Childs' invitation to Rand to follow her ideas to what he sees as their logical conclusion and convert to free-market anarchism. Childs explains that he thinks Rand is wrong in advocating a limited government, that the state is a moral evil which should not be tolerated even in limited form.[39] Rand was not convinced; Childs' name was removed from *The Objectivist* mailing list. Childs was undaunted. When Rand died, he called her "a powerful voice for liberty" and wrote about her important contributions to the Libertarian movement.[40] Childs lauds her impact: "The point is that no one said it the way Ayn Rand did, with the force of a small but potent nuke."

Since her death *The Objectivist Forum* has carried a series of articles assessing Rand's significance in such fields as philosophy, economics, education, psychology and journalism. These are articles of eulogy, containing neither extended discussion nor proof.

REVIEWS

Criticism has had negligible effect on the popularity of Ayn Rand's works. Over the years there have been those few reviewers who have appreciated not only Rand's writing style but also her message. Their number is far outweighed by those who have been everything from hysterically hostile to merely uncomprehending. The antagonism of critical reaction grew in direct proportion to the enthusiasm of the reading public.

Rand's first novel did not burst on the literary scene with much fanfare. The reviewer for *The Christian Century* found it "vigorous" and emotionally intense and the characters' motivations clearly drawn, but there is no indication in the composite review, which includes *We the Living* with *Norma Darrell* by Beverley R. Tucker and *The Yankee Bodleys* by Naomi Lane Babson, that Lee E. Cannon found this book, still in print nearly a half-century later, significantly different from the other two, now obscure.[41] Ben Belitt juxtaposes *We the Living* and Alexei Tolstoi's *Darkness and Dawn* as two novels about Russia. Belitt is not convinced that Rand's depiction of the situation in Russia is accurate, but claims he does not want to quarrel with her politics; what he does take exception to is Kira as a spokesperson. He finds no reason, in Kira's actions, to respect her judgment; the plot is described as shuttling about "aimlessly from bedroom to rostrum."[42]

One year earlier, the opening of *Night of January 16th* had not been a critical triumph either. Brooks Atkinson, the *New York Times'* formidable reviewer, found it "routine theatre with the usual brew of hokum."[43] A revival, thirty-eight years later, under the original title *Penthouse Legend*, was treated even less hospitably by Clive Barnes. Barnes calls the drama boring and tedious, the writing murky, the acting not particularly good.[44] At least Walter Pidgeon got good reviews in the original production.

Rand's dramatic power and passionate intensity are recognized by both sympathetic and hostile reviewers. The sympathetic reviewers find that these qualities sweep them along; their interest never flags. N. L. Rothman describes the writing in *The Fountainhead* as "strong, dramatic, everywhere intense and highly articulate." He compares it to Sinclair Lewis' *Arrowsmith* in ideals and satiric attack.[45] The *New York Times* reviewer characterizes Rand's writings as brilliant, beautiful and bitter.[46] Like Rothman, she recognizes that *The Fountainhead* is a novel of ideas. Negative reviewers scorn Rand's intensity as overwrought and her drama as melodramatic.

Another recurring criticism of *The Fountainhead* is its length. The *Library Journal* calls it "well written but too long."[47] Diana Trilling calls it "the curiosity of the year" and suggests that anyone who buys it "deserves a stern lecture on paper-rationing."[48] It was published during World War II when many items, including paper, were in short supply. Rand was obviously unconcerned with such fault-finding; her next novel, *Atlas Shrugged*, is almost twice as long.

Though the book was enthusiastically received by some important reviewers, the movie of *The Fountainhead* met nearly universal disapprobation. Released in 1949, some six years after the book's publication, the movie could rely on a pre-sold audience which had ignored the negative criticisms, if indeed they had read them, and put the book on the list of best-sellers. Bosley Crowther disapproves of not only the acting— Patricia Neal's is called "affected" and Gary Cooper's "slightly pathetic"—but he also finds the reasoning specious. He cannot understand how Roark's participation in a fraudulent scheme is that much less culpable than Peter Keating's.[49] Reacting with characteristic derision, *Time's* caustic critic claims that the title of *The Fountainhead* is an understatement; he thinks it should be called a "geyser of emotional sounds and ideological fury." He damns the dialog, calling it muddleheaded, stagy, and pretentious.[50] Even the usually gentle *Good Housekeeping*, which concedes the importance of Rand's theme, wishes the movie had presented it more entertainingly and with more vitality.[51]

By the time *Atlas Shrugged* was published Ayn Rand had begun to surround herself with a coterie of admiring readers. Many fans of *The Fountainhead* anxiously awaited the publication of their favorite author's next book. From the fury of the fusillades leveled against it, one might think that an army of detractors was also waiting, lying in ambush. Some of the venom is predictable; Rand's antipathy to William F. Buckley and his ilk was well known. Whittaker Chambers lambasts *Atlas Shrugged* in a lengthy article for the *National Review*. Chambers faults the "dictatorial tone," "overriding arrogance," unreprieved "shrillness," and "total absence of any saving humor."[52] With equal fervor and a more vehement vocabulary, the *Atlantic Monthly* reviewer calls the book "execrable claptrap" and a "solemn grotesquerie."[53] Other reviewers seemed to vie with each other in a contest to devise the cleverest put-downs; *Time* opened its review with "Is it a novel? Is it a nightmare? Is it Superman—in the comic-strip or the Nietzschean version?"[54]

Granville Hicks in the *New York Times* was put off by what he perceived as the misanthropy that Rand demonstrates in her gleeful destruction of the world. Hicks says "the book is written out of hate."[55] Helen Beal Woodward's evaluation parallels Hicks'. "The book is shot through with hatred," says Woodward, and then lists moralists, mystics, professors, evangelists, communists, altruists, and bureaucrats as among those that Rand hates. Though Woodward admires Rand's writing abilities—calling her a writer of "dazzling virtuosity"—she feels that Rand wastes her writing gifts by her remorseless hectoring and prolixity.[56]

Atlas Shrugged was not without its critical admirers. John Chamberlain is overwhelmed by the enormity of the task of reviewing such a monumental work. He sees it as a book to satisfy any number of tastes and compares it to Buck Rogers as science fiction and Dostoevsky as a "philosophical detective story," and admires both its "Socratic dialog" and "profound political parable."[57] Richard McLaughlin compares Atlas Shrugged to Uncle Tom's Cabin in terms of political importance. He is not overfond of Rand's "long-windedness," but he admires her skillful polemics.[58]

After Atlas Shrugged Rand published no more fiction. Though they sell well, none of her nonfiction works approaches her fiction in sales. Nor was any of her nonfiction works accorded the same amount of critical attention as Atlas Shrugged. Some of the critics of For the New Intellectual approved of the idea of gathering all of the main philosophical speeches of Rand's novels into one book; others thought it repetitious. Many of the same charges that were leveled against her novels were repeated against this compilation from them. Several of the reviews of The Virtue of Selfishness point out the similarities between Rand's philosophy and Existentialism.[59] Noting that Capitalism: The Unknown Ideal is a "mélange" from other sources, the Library Journal recommends the book be bought only by those libraries in which Rand is in demand.[60] The Freeman's review is appreciative of Rand's "unique arguments" and her explosion of many anticapitalist myths.[61] Honor Tracy titles her review of the same book "Here We Go Gathering Nuts" and compares Rand to those fervent lunatics, in particular the ones who alone knew what was wrong with mankind, that declaimed their views on Speakers' Corner in Hyde Park.[62] Rand's last works, including the one published posthumously, received little critical attention except in specialized newsletters and journals.

NOTES

1. The character, Mr. A, is derived from Rand's articulation of the philosophical premise that A = A, the title of Part III of Atlas Shrugged.

2. The contemporary rock group Rush's 1976 album 2112 reads, "With acknowledgment to the genius of Ayn Rand."

3. "Break Free!" Reason, October 1971, p. 9.

4. Interview with Barbara Branden, Los Angeles, 9 Nov. 1981.

5. Albert Ellis, Is Objectivism a Religion? (New York: Lyle Stuart, Inc., 1968), p. 70.

6. "Break Free!" p. 14.

7. William F. O'Neill, *With Charity toward None* (New York: Philosophical Library, 1971), p. 14.

8. John W. Robbins, *Answer to Ayn Rand: A Critique of the Philosophy of Objectivism* (Washington, D.C.: Mt. Vernon Publishing Co., Inc., 1974), p. 12.

9. Douglas J. Den Uyl and Douglas B. Rasmussen, *The Philosophical Thought of Ayn Rand* (Champagne/Urbana: University of Illinois Press, 1984), p. 4.

10. Wallace Matson, "Rand on Concepts," in *The Philosophical Thought of Ayn Rand*, p. 19.

11. Nora Ephron, "A Strange Kind of Simplicity," *New York Times Book Review*, 5 May 1968, p. 8.

12. Barbara Grizzuti Harrison, "Psyching Out Ayn Rand," *Ms.* September 1978, p. 34.

13. Bruce Cook, "Ayn Rand: A Voice in the Wilderness," *Catholic World*, May 1965, p. 124. At one point Cook says that the Rand mystique may "prove more attractive than that tired old Norse paganism revived by Paul Joseph Goebbels."

14. John Kobler, "The Curious Cult of Ayn Rand," *Saturday Evening Post*, 11 Nov. 1961, p. 98.

15. Robert L. White, "Ayn Rand—Hipster on the Right," *New University Thought* 2 (Autumn 1962): 61.

16. Jeff Riggenbach, "The Disowned Children of Ayn Rand," *Reason*, December 1982, p. 59.

17. Terminology is important in Randian circles. As Rand was very zealous about the purity of her ideas and did not want people claiming they were Objectivists when their ideas might differ from hers, she issued "A Statement of Policy" in which she defined Objectivism and delineated the only authentic sources. She then warned against people attempting to act as "spokesmen for Objectivism." Her lawyer Henry Mark Holzer suggested that people who were supporters or interested in learning more about Rand's philosophy should identify themselves as "students of Objectivism." The editor's note in a recent issue of *The Objectivist Forum* (February 1983) states: "The phrase 'students of Objectivism' was originally introduced to avoid implicitly ascribing to Ayn Rand herself the ideas of her followers and admirers. Now that Miss Rand is no longer alive, this phrase has become unnecessary, and I am dropping it. I will henceforth use the term 'Objectivists' not in an honorific sense but simply to designate those who advocate the philosophy of Objectivism."

18. Nora Sayre, "The Cult of Ayn Rand," *New Statesman*, 11 March 1966, p. 332.

19. "Break Free!" p. 10.

20. Dora Jane Hamblin, "The Cult of Angry Ayn Rand," *Life*, 7 April 1967, p. 101.

21. "Born Eccentric," *Newsweek*, 17 March 1961, p. 105.

22. Tamara Stadnychenko, "*Anthem*: A Book for All Reasons," *English Journal* 72 (February 1983): 77.

23. Mimi Gladstein, "Ayn Rand and Feminism: An Unlikely Alliance," *College English* 39 (February 1978): 26.

24. Paul Deane, "Ayn Rand's Neurotic Personalities of Our Times," *Revue des Langues Vivantes* 36 (1970): 125.

25. Philip Gordon, "The Extroflective Hero: A Look at Ayn Rand," *Journal of Popular Culture* 10 (Spring 1977): 701.

26. Both of these articles as well as Douglas Den Uyl's "The New Republic" which compares *Atlas Shrugged* to Plato's *Republic* appear in the November 1973 issue of *Reason*. Another article, not related to Rand's literary works, George Smith's "Atheism and Objectivism," is the fourth article in this special issue dedicated to Ayn Rand.

27. Norman P. Barry, "The New Liberalism," *British Journal of Political Science* 13 (January 1983): 105–10.

28. Robert Nozick, "On the Randian Argument," *Personalist* 52 (Spring 1971): 282–304.

29. Tibor Machan, "Nozick and Rand on Property Rights," *Personalist* 58 (April 1977): 192–95.

30. Douglas Den Uyl and Douglas Rasmussen, "Nozick on the Randian Argument," *Personalist* 59 (April 1978): 184–205.

31. George T. Mavrodes, "Property," *Personalist* 53 (Summer 1972): 245–62.

32. Stephen E. Taylor, "Is Ayn Rand Selfish, or Only Confused?" *Journal of Thought* 4 (January 1969): 12–29.

33. Kenneth Smith, "Ayn Rand: Objectivism or Existentialism," *Religious Humanism* 4 (Winter 1970): 23–28.

34. Hazel Barnes, *An Existentialist Ethics* (New York: Alfred E. Knopf, 1967) pp. 124–49.

35. Barnes, p. 125.

36. Barnes, pp. 141–46.

37. Tibor Machan, "Editorial Introduction: The Significance of Ayn Rand," *Reason*, (November 1973), p. 5.

38. Tibor Machan, "Ayn Rand: A Contemporary Heretic?" *The Occasional Review* 4 (Winter 1976): 133–50.

39. Roy A. Childs, Jr., "An Open Letter to Ayn Rand," *Rational Individualist*, August 1969.

40. Roy A. Childs, Jr., "Ayn Rand and the Libertarian Movement," *Update On the Libertarian Movement* 2 (April 1982): 4.

41. Lee E. Cannon, "The Quick and the Dead," *The Christian Century*, 1 July 1936, p. 941.

42. Ben Belitt, "The Red and the White," *The Nation*, 22 April 1936, pp. 522–24.

43. Brooks Atkinson, review in *New York Times*, 17 Sept. 1935, p. 26, col. 4.

44. Clive Barnes, " 'Penthouse Legend,' A Courtroom Drama," *New York Times*, 23 Feb. 1973, p. 20, col. 1.

45. N. L. Rothman, "H. Roark, Architect," *Saturday Review of Literature*, 29 May 1943, p. 30.

46. Lorine Pruette, "Battle against Evil," *New York Times Book Review*, 16 May 1943, p. 7.

47. Felix E. Hirsch, review in *Library Journal*, 15 April 1943, p. 328.

48. Diana Trilling, "Fiction in Review," *The Nation*, 12 June 1943, p. 843.

49. Bosley Crowther, "Gary Cooper Plays an Idealistic Architect in Film Version of 'The Fountainhead,' " *New York Times*, 9 July 1949, p. 8, col. 5.

50. *Time*, 11 July 1949, p. 95.

51. *Good Housekeeping*, July 1949, p. 200.

52. Whittaker Chambers, "Big Sister Is Watching You," *National Review*, 28 Dec. 1957, p. 596.

53. Charles Rolo, "Comes the Revolution," *Atlantic Monthly*, November 1957, p. 249.

54. "The Solid-Gold Dollar Sign," *Time*, 14 Oct. 1957, p. 128.

55. Granville Hicks, "A Parable of Buried Talents," *New York Times Book Review*, 13 Oct. 1957, p. 5.

56. Helen Beal Woodward, "Non-Stop Daydream," *Saturday Review*, 12 Oct. 1957, p. 25.

57. John Chamberlain, "Ayn Rand's Political Parable and Thundering Melodrama," *New York Herald Tribune*, 6 Oct. 1957, sec. 6, p. 1.

58. Richard McLaughlin, "The Lady Has a Message . . . ," *The American Mercury*, January 1958, pp. 144–46.

59. The reviewer for *Choice*, 2 April 1965, p. 100, says that Rand is "an odd kind of existentialist." Vincent J. Colimore suggests in his review in *Best Sellers*, 1 Jan. 1966, p. 387, that Rand's philosophy resembles the "Existentialist tenets of Camus, Sartre et al."

60. Jack VanDerhoof, *Library Journal*, 1 Dec. 1966, p. 5984.

61. Elizabeth Gillett, "Other Books," *The Freeman* 17, no. 3 (March 1967): 189–90.

62. Honor Tracy, "Here We Go Gathering Nuts," *New Republic*, 10 Dec. 1966, p. 27.

Works Reviewed Positively by Objectivist Publications

What follows is a listing of some works that have been positively reviewed in Objectivist publications. While Rand did not necessarily agree with all the premises of the authors included on this list, she did think enough of these works to have them reviewed in her newsletters and/or to offer them for sale through the Nathaniel Branden Institute Book Service and The Objectivist Book Service.

Abbreviations: The Objectivist Newsletter — ON
                      The Objectivist — O

Anderson, Benjamin M. *Economics and the Public Welfare: Financial and Economic History of the United States, 1914–1946.* ON-May 1965
Barzun, Jacques. *The American University.* O-November, 1968
Beck, Joan. *How To Raise a Brighter Child.* O-September 1968
Blanshard, Brand. *Reason and Analysis.* ON-February 1963
Chu, Valentin. *Ta Ta, Tan Tan.* ON-November 1963
Crane, Philip M. *The Democrat's Dilemma.* ON-October 1965
Crocker, George N. *Roosevelt's Road to Russia.* ON-January 1964
Drury, Allen. *Preserve and Protect.* O-December 1968
Ekirch, Arthur, Jr. *The Decline of American Liberalism.* ON-July 1962
Fertig, Lawrence. *Prosperity through Freedom.* ON-March 1962
Fleming, Harold. *Ten Thousand Commandments.* ON-April 1962
Flynn, John T. *The Roosevelt Myth.* ON-December 1962
Friedan, Betty. *The Feminine Mystique.* ON-July 1963
Gish, Lillian. *The Movies, Mr. Griffith, and Me.* O-November 1969
Hacker, Louis M. *The World of Andrew Carnegie.* O-April 1969
Hainstock, Elizabeth. *Teaching Montessori in the Home.* O-July 1971
Hazlitt, Henry. *Economics in One Lesson.* ON-February 1962
Hoffman, Banesh. *The Tyranny of Testing.* ON-March 1964
Hugo, Victor. *Ninety-Three.* ON-October 1962
Jones, W. T. *A History of Western Philosophy.* ON-September 1964
Kaufmann, Walter. *Philosophic Classics.* ON-September 1964

Keller, Werner. *East Minus West = Zero.* ON-November 1962

Lyons, Eugene. *Workers' Paradise Lost.* O-January 1968

Marchenko, Anatoly. *My Testimony.* O-July 1970

Mason, Lowell B. *The Language of Dissent.* ON-August 1963

Montessori, Maria. *Dr. Montessori's Own Handbook.* O-July 1970

Paterson, Isabel. *The God of the Machine.* ON-October 1964

Randall, John Herman, Jr. *Aristotle.* ON-May 1963

Rattigan, Terence. *Plays*, Vol. II

———. *Separate Tables*

———. *The Winslow Boy*

Scheibla, Shirley. *Poverty Is Where the Money Is.* O-August 1969

Spillane, Mickey. *The Girl Hunters.* ON-October 1962

Sutton, Anthony C. *Western Technology and Soviet Economic Development, 1917 to 1930.* O-January 1970

Toledano, Ralph de. *The Greatest Plot in History.* ON-May 1964

Von Mises, Ludwig. *The Anti-Capitalist Mentality.* ON-May 1962

———. *Bureaucracy*

———. *Human Action*, revised edition. ON-September 1963

———. *Omnipotent Government.* O-August 1970

———. *Planned Chaos.* ON-January 1962

———. *Planning for Freedom.* ON-September 1962

Windelband, Wilhelm. A *History of Philosophy.* ON-September 1964

Bibliography

What follows is as comprehensive a bibliography on Ayn Rand as has been published to date. Both the serious academic researcher and the merely curious reader should find it more than sufficient as a reference resource. However, it is not exhaustive. A definitive bibliography would be the subject of a book in and of itself.

This *Companion* is designed to be useful in the average library. If I missed certain esoteric sources, it is because general reference sources did not index them and computer searches did not unearth them. There are sources, such as privately published pamphlets, organization newsletters or articles in popular journals, that are not available through normal avenues of library research. Most libraries carry a limited number of newspaper indexes. The newsletters of various Objectivist and Libertarian institutions or groups are not generally indexed. In cases where such materials have become known to me, I have included them. However, there is much that may have eluded my search.

The Bibliography is organized for maximum research efficiency. Part I includes the primary sources, that is, the words of Rand herself. In this section I have tried to avoid redundancy. Separately published articles or pamphlets that were also published in the Objectivist periodicals and later as parts of books are usually not listed separately. While all the publications of Rand's writings to date are included, the listings of speeches and of radio and television appearances are limited. Beginning in the 1960s, Rand was a popular lecturer and public figure who made a number of appearances on various talk-show programs such as the Les Crane show and the Johnny Carson show ("Tonight") as well as on a number of college campuses. She was interviewed by Mike Wallace and Edwin Newman, among others. Cataloging all such appearances is beyond the scope of this study though I have included some of the appearances that are accessible via tapes or transcripts. *The Objectivist Forum* has announced plans to publish excerpts from Rand's unpublished works in a series which will run through December of 1984. I have included those that are available as of this writing.

Part II of this Bibliography is composed of books, articles, reviews, letters, speeches and other materials written by others about Ayn Rand and her work. This part also contains a section on the reference dictionaries, guides and encyclopedias that include an entry on Rand or a mention of her place in contemporary literature. Obituaries are listed with the reference articles.

The next section of the Bibliography, Part III, is composed of representative materials of tangential interest, such as articles or books that are essentially about other matters or individuals but that contain a reference to Ayn Rand. In some cases this reference is substantial; in others it is no more than an acknowledgment in a footnote. However, these sources are important in that they help illustrate the extent of her contemporary impact. For those who are interested in Ivar Kreuger, the reporting of whose suicide was the occasion for the writing of *Night of January 16th*, I have included some items about him in Part IV.

PART I: WORKS BY RAND

Books

Anthem. London: Cassell and Company, 1938. Revised edition, Los Angeles: Pamphleteers, Inc., 1946; Caldwell, Idaho: The Caxton Printers, 1953. Paperback: New York: New American Library, 1946.

Atlas Shrugged. New York: Random House, 1957. Paperback: New York: New American Library, 1957.

Capitalism: The Unknown Ideal. New York: New American Library, 1966. Paperback: New York: New American Library, 1967.

For the New Intellectual. New York: Random House, 1961. Paperback: New York: New American Library, 1961.

The Fountainhead. New York: The Bobbs-Merrill Company, 1943. Paperback: New York: New American Library, 1952.

Introduction to Objectivist Epistemology. New York: New American Library, 1979. Paperback only.

The New Left: The Anti-Industrial Revolution. New York: New American Library, 1971. Paperback only.

Night of January 16th. New York: Longmans, Green, 1936. Paperback: New York: World Publishing Co., 1968; New York: New American Library, 1971.

Philosophy: Who Needs It? New York: The Bobbs-Merrill Company, Inc., 1982.

The Romantic Manifesto. New York: The World Publishing Company, 1969. Paperback: New York: New American Library, 1971.

The Unconquered. (Typewritten play manuscript—unpublished.) Adaptation of *We the Living*. First New York production, Biltmore Theatre, Feb. 13, 1940.

The Virtue of Selfishness. New York: New American Library, 1964. Paperback only.

We the Living. New York: The Macmillan Company, 1936; London: Cassell, 1937; New York: Random House, 1959. Paperback: New York: New American Library, 1959.

Newsletters

Ayn Rand et al. *The Objectivist Newsletter*. Volumes 1–4. New York: The Objectivist, Inc., 1962–65.

————. *The Objectivist*. Volumes 5–10. New York: The Objectivist, Inc., 1966–71.

Ayn Rand and Leonard Peikoff. *The Ayn Rand Letter*. Volumes 1–4. New York: The Ayn Rand Letter, Inc., 1971–76.

Articles, Short Stories, Letters

"Ayn Rand Explains." Letter. *New York Times*, 11 Aug. 1976, p. 34, col. 5.

"Ayn Rand Replies to Criticism of Her Film." Letter. *New York Times*, 24 July 1949, sec. 2, p. 4, col. 1.

Introduction. *Calumet "K"* by Merwin-Webster. Originally published New York: Macmillan Co., 1901; version with Rand introduction reissued by Palo Alto Book Service, 1983.

Introduction. *The God of the Machine* by Isabel Paterson. Originally published New York: G. P. Putnam's Sons, 1943; 1964 version with Rand introduction published in Caldwell, Idaho, by Caxton Printers; reissued by Palo Alto Book Service, Palo Alto, Calif., 1983.

Introduction. *The Ominous Parallels* by Leonard Peikoff. New York: Stein and Day, 1982.

Introduction. *Ninety-Three* by Victor Hugo, translated by Lowell Bair. New York: Bantam Books, Inc., 1962; reissued by Palo Alto Book Service, 1983.

"J.F.K.—High Class Beatnik?" *Human Events*, 17 (1 Sept. 1960): 393–94.

"Let Us Alone!" *Yale Political Magazine*, Summer 1964.

"The Money-Making Personality." *Cosmopolitan*, April 1963, pp. 37–41.

"The New Left Represents an Intellectual Vacuum." *New York Times Magazine*, 17 May 1970, pp. 113, 116.

"The Only Path to Tomorrow." *Reader's Digest*, January 1944, pp. 88–90.

"A Screen Guide For Americans." *Plain Talk*, November 1947, pp. 37–42.

"Textbook of Americanism." *The Vigil*, 1946.

"Why I Like Stamp Collecting." *Minkus Stamp Journal* 6, no. 2 (1971): 2–5.

Ayn Rand, Ralph Nader, et al. "Do Our Tax Laws Need a Shake-up?" *Saturday Review of the Society* 55, no. 43 (November 1972): 45–52.

Radio Programs and Television Appearances

"Ayn Rand on Campus," Station WKCR-FM, New York City, Columbia University, 1 March–17 May 1962.

Ayn Rand—Two Radio Talks. "The Money-Making Personality" and "The Brain Drain." Cassette available from Palo Alto Book Service.

"Commentary," Station WBAI-FM, New York City, beginning 27 April 1965.

"Donahue," WGN-TV, Chicago, Illinois, 29 April 1965.

"Donahue," WGN-TV, Chicago, Illinois, May 1979. (Broadcast from Madison Square Garden, New York City.)

An Interview with Ayn Rand, Raymond Newman, interviewer. Cassette available from Palo Alto Book Service.

Speaking Freely: Edwin Newman Interviews Ayn Rand. Cassette available from Palo Alto Book Service.

"Tomorrow," Tom Snyder, host. NBC-TV, 2 July 1979.

Translations

These are the translations listed in the *National Union Catalog* and therefore easily accessible in major libraries.

Atlas Shrugged

La Rebelión de Atlas, transl. Julio Fernandez-Yanez. Barcelona: Caralt, 1961.

The Fountainhead

Der ewige Quell, transl. Harry Kahn. Zurich: Morgarten-Verlag, 1946.
La Fonte Meravigliosa, transl. Giangi Colombo Taccani and Maria Silvi. Milan: Baldini & Castoldi, n.d.
El Manantial, transl. Luis de Paola. Barcelona: Editorial Planeta, 1966.
La Source Vive, transl. Jane Fillion. Geneva: J. H. Jeheber, 1945.

Night of January 16th

La Nuit du 16 Janvier, transl. Marcel Dubois. Paris: Editions Billaudot, 1946.

We the Living

Los Que Vivimos, transl. Fernando Acevedo. Mexico: Editorial Diana, 1965.
Vi, der lever, transl. Else Brudenell-Bruce. Copenhagen: Berlingske forlag, 1946.

Miscellaneous

Column. *Los Angeles Times*. (Weekly from 17 June 1962 to 16 December 1962.)
"Conservativism: An Obituary." (Speech delivered at Princeton University, 7 Dec. 1960.)
"Faith and Force: Destroyers of the Modern World," *Vital Speeches* 26 (1 August 1960): 630–36.
"The Fascist New Frontier." (Lecture delivered at Ford Hall Forum, Boston, 16 Dec. 1962.)
"From Ayn Rand's Unpublished Writings: Philosophical Journal," ed. Harry Binswanger, *The Objectivist Forum*, August 1983, pp. 1–8.
"From Ayn Rand's Unpublished Writings: Roark and Cameron," ed. Harry Binswanger, *The Objectivist Forum*, April 1983, pp. 1–10.
"*Playboy* Interview: Ayn Rand," Alvin Toffler, interviewer, *Playboy*, March 1964, pp. 35–43.
"The Sanction of the Victim." (Speech delivered at the National Committee on Monetary Reform Conference, New Orleans, Louisiana, 18–22 Nov. 1981.) Rand's last public appearance is available in both audio and video tape.

PART II: WORKS ABOUT RAND

Books

Branden, Barbara and Nathaniel Branden. *Who Is Ayn Rand?* New York: Random House, 1962. Paperback: New York: Paperback Library, Inc., 1964.

Den Uyl, Douglas and Douglas Rasmussen, eds. *The Philosophical Thought of Ayn Rand*. Chicago: University of Illinois Press, 1984.

Ellis, Albert. *Is Objectivism a Religion?* New York: Lyle Stuart, Inc., 1968.

Lepanto, Paul. *Return to Reason*. New York: Exposition Press, 1971.

O'Neill, William. *With Charity Toward None: An Analysis of Ayn Rand's Philosophy*. New York: Philosophical Library, 1971.

Robbins, John W. *Answer to Ayn Rand: A Critique of the Philosophy of Objectivism*. Washington, D.C.: Mt. Vernon Publishing Co., 1974.

Tuccille, Jerome. *It Usually Begins with Ayn Rand*. New York: Stein and Day, 1972.

Articles in Books, Magazines, Journals, Newsletters and Newspapers

" 'Atlas' Rolling." *Frontlines* 1, no. 3 (November 1978): 1.

" 'Atlas' Contest Bombs." *Frontlines* 1, no. 8 (April 1979): 1, 5.

" 'Atlas' May Rise Again." *Frontlines* 2, no. 1 (September 1979): 1–2.

"Author Wins Royalty Row." *New York Times*, 11 Feb. 1936, p. 19.

"Ayn Rand Reports to S.E.C. Hearings." *New York Times*, 9 Sept. 1958, p. 23, col. 3.

"Ayn Rand Returns." *Look*, 14 May 1979, pp. 72–73.

Barnes, Hazel E. "Egoistic Humanism: Ayn Rand's Objectivism." In *An Existentialist Ethics*, New York: Alfred A. Knopf, 1967, pp. 124–29.

Berliner, Michael S. "Ayn Rand and Education." *The Objectivist Forum*, August 1982, pp. 10–13.

Binswanger, Harry. "Ayn Rand's Philosophic Achievement." *The Objectivist Forum*, June 1982, pp. 8–13.

———. "Ayn Rand's Philosophic Achievement, Part II." *The Objectivist Forum*, August 1982, pp. 1–3.

———. "Ayn Rand's Philosophic Achievement, Part III." *The Objectivist Forum*, October 1982, pp. 1–4.

———. "Ayn Rand's Philosophic Achievement, Part IV." *The Objectivist Forum*, December 1982, pp. 1–12.

Bissell, Roger. "Resolving the Government Issue." *Reason*, November 1973, pp. 26–29.

"Books into Films." *Publishers Weekly*, 30 Sept. 1944, 1418.

"Born Eccentric." *Newsweek*, 27 March 1961, pp. 104–5.

Branden, Nathaniel. "Thank You Ayn Rand, and Goodbye." *Reason*, May 1978, pp. 58–61.

Buechner, M. Northrup. "Ayn Rand and Economics." *The Objectivist Forum*, August 1982, pp. 3–9.

"The Chairman's Favorite Author." *Time*, 30 Sept. 1974, pp. 87–88.

Childs, R. A., Jr. "The Contradiction of Objectivism." *Rampart Journal of Individualist Thought* 4, no. 1 (Spring 1968): 84.

———. "An Open Letter to Ayn Rand: Objectivism and the State." *Rational Individualist*, August 1969.

Cody, John. "Ayn Rand's Promethean Heroes." *Reason*, November 1973, pp. 30–35.

Collins, James. "Ayn Rand's Talents for Getting Headlines." *America* 105 (29 July 1961): 569.

Collins, Kathleen. "The Girder and the Trellis." *Reason*, November 1973, pp. 13–16.

Cook, Bruce. "Ayn Rand: A Voice in the Wilderness." *Catholic World*, May 1965, pp. 119–24.

Cory, Steven. "Rerouting Ayn Rand's 'Virtue of Selfishness.' " *Christianity Today* 26 (18 June 1982): 72.

"Court Upholds Use of Author's Name in Blurb." *Publishers Weekly*, 31 March 1969, p. 35.

Deane, Paul. "Ayn Rand's Neurotic Personalities of Our Times." *Revue des Langues Vivantes* 36 (1970): 125–29.

Den Uyl, Douglas. "The New Republic." *Reason*, November 1973, pp. 6–11.

Den Uyl, Douglas and Douglas Rasmussen. "Nozick on the Randian Argument." *Personalist* 59 (April 1978): 184–205.

"Disturber of the Peace: Ayn Rand." *Mademoiselle*, May 1962, pp. 172–73, 194–96.

"Down with Altruism." *Time*, 29 Feb. 1960, pp. 94–95.

Ephron, Nora. "A Strange Kind of Simplicity." *New York Times Book Review*, 5 May 1968, p. 8+.

Evans, M. Stanton. "The Gospel According to Ayn Rand." *National Review*, 3 Oct. 1967, pp. 1059–63.

Fletcher, Max E. "Harriet Martineau and Ayn Rand: Economics in the Guise of Fiction." *American Journal of Economics and Sociology* 33, no. 4 (October 1974): 367–79.

————. "A Rejoinder." *American Journal of Economics and Sociology* 35, no. 2 (April 1976): 224.

Gladstein, Mimi R. "Ayn Rand and Feminism: An Unlikely Alliance." *College English* 39, no. 6 (Feb. 1978): 25–30.

Gordon, Philip. "The Extroflective Hero: A Look at Ayn Rand." *Journal of Popular Culture* 10, no. 4 (Spring 1977): 701–10.

Hamblin, Dora Jane. "The Cult of Angry Ayn Rand." *Life*, 7 April 1967, pp. 92–102.

Hanscom, Leslie. "Lecture Circuit: Born Eccentric." *Newsweek*, 27 March 1961, pp. 104–5.

Harrison, Barbara Grizzuti. "Psyching Out Ayn Rand." *Ms.*, September 1978, pp. 24–34.

Hunt, Robert. "Science Fiction for the Age of Inflation: Reading *Atlas Shrugged* in the 1980s," in George E. Slusser, Eric S. Rabkin, and Robert Scholes, eds., *Coordinates: Placing Science Fiction and Fantasy. Alternative Series*, Joseph D. Olander, general editor. Carbondale and Edwardsville: Southern Illinois University Press, 1984, pp. 80–98.

Kobler, John. "The Curious Cult of Ayn Rand." *The Saturday Evening Post*, 11 Nov. 1961, pp. 98–101.

Kornstein, Daniel. "Ayn Rand's Legal World." In *The Music of the Laws*, pp. 89–93. New York: Everest House, 1982.

Lennox, James G. "Fletcher's Oblique Attack on Ayn Rand's Economics and Ethics." *American Journal of Economics and Sociology* 35, no. 2 (April 1976): 217–24.

Letwin, William. "A Credo for the Ultras." *The Reporter*, October 1962, pp. 56–62.

Locke, Edwin A. "Ayn Rand and Psychology." *The Objectivist Forum*, October 1982, pp. 5–8.

————. "Ayn Rand and Psychology." *The Objectivist Forum*, December 1982, pp. 12–15.

Machan, Tibor R. "Ayn Rand: A Contemporary Heretic?" *The Occasional Review* 4 (Winter 1976): 133–49.

————. "Editorial Introduction: The Significance of Ayn Rand." *Reason*, November 1973, p. 5.

————. "Nozick and Rand on Property Rights." *Personalist* 58 (April 1977): 192–95.

McGann, Kevin. "Ayn Rand and the Stockyard of the Spirit." In *The Modern American Novel and the Movies*, Gerald Peary and Roger Shatzkin, eds. New York: Frederick Ungar Publishing Co., 1978.

"NBC Drops 'Atlas.' " *Frontlines* 1, no. 10 (June 1979): 1, 5.

Nathan, Paul S. "Books into Films." *Publishers Weekly*, 11 June 1949, p. 2405.

Nichols, Lewis. "Class of '43." *New York Times Book Review*, 22 Dec. 1967, p. 8.

————. "Talk with Ayn Rand." *New York Times Book Review*, 13 Oct. 1957, p. 16.

"Note on a Bestseller." *Commonweal*, 3 Jan. 1958, p. 349.

Nozick, Robert. "On the Randian Argument." *Personalist* 52 (Spring 1971): 282–304.

O'Quinn, Kerry. "Ayn Rand's Heroism." *Starlog* 59 (June 1982).

Peikoff, Leonard. "Ayn Rand." *The Objectivist Forum*, June 1982, pp. 1–3.

"People." *Time*, 12 Jan. 1976, p. 32.

Pilpel, Harriet F. and Kenneth P. Norwick. "Can You Name an Author in a Blurb?" *Publishers Weekly*, 5 May 1969, pp. 23–24.

"Rand Announces 'Atlas' TV Project." *Frontlines* 4, no. 4 (Dec. 1981): 1, 3.

"Rand Blasts Reaganites." *Frontlines* 3, no. 9 (June 1981): p. 1.

"Rand Charms Snyder." *Frontlines* 1, no. 12 (Aug. 1979): 3, 6.

"Rand Interviewed." *Frontlines* 2, no. 10 (July 1980): 2.

"Rand on Donahue." *Frontlines* 1, no. 10 (June 1979): 3.

"Reagan's Randians." *Frontlines* 3, no. 3 (Nov. 1980): 2.

Ridpath, John B. "Fletcher's Views of the Novelist's Aesthetic Purpose in Writing." *American Journal of Economics and Sociology* 35, no. 2 (April 1976): 211–17.

Riggenbach, Jeff. "The Disowned Children of Ayn Rand." *Reason*, December 1982, pp. 57–59.

St. John, Jeffrey. "Are American Students Flunking Capitalism?" *Nation's Business*, July 1967, p. 90.

Sayre, Nora. "The Cult of Ayn Rand." *New Statesman*, 11 March 1966, p. 332.

Schroder, Charles Frederick. "Ayn Rand: Far Right Prophetess." *Christian Century* 78 (13 Dec. 1961): 1493–95.

Schwartz, Jerry. "Ayn Rand and Journalism," *The Objectivist Forum*, October 1982, pp. 8–13.

———. "Interview with Ayn Rand." *The Objectivist Forum*, June 1980, pp. 1–6.

———. "Interview with Ayn Rand, Part II." *The Objectivist Forum*, August 1980, pp. 1–3.

"Second Arbitration on Play Royalties." *New York Times*, 17 Jan. 1936, p. 15.

Smith, George. "Atheism and Objectivism." *Reason*, November 1973, pp. 18–24.

Smith, Kenneth. "Ayn Rand: Objectivism or Existentialism." *Religious Humanism* 4 (Winter 1970): 23–28.

Stadnychenko, Tamara. "*Anthem*: A Book for All Reasons." *English Journal* 72, no. 2 (February 1983): 77–78.

"A Steel House with a Suave Finish." *House and Garden*, August 1949, pp. 54–57.

Taylor, Stephen E. "Is Ayn Rand Really Selfish, or Only Confused?" *Journal of Thought* 4 (January 1969): 12–29.

"TIA's Interview with Leonard Peikoff." In *The Battle for Laissez-Faire Capitalism*, ed. Peter Schwartz, pp. 56–64. New York: The Intellectual Activist, 1983.

White, Robert L. "Ayn Rand—Hipster on the Right." *New University Thought* 2 (Autumn 1962): 57–72.

"Who Will Play in 'Atlas': A Frontlines Casting Contest." *Frontlines* 1, no. 5 (January 1979): 6.

Reviews of Rand's Fiction

Anthem

"Briefer Mention." *Freeman*, 21 Sept. 1953, p. 931.

Atlas Shrugged

Blackman, Ruth Chapin. "Controversial Books by Ayn Rand and Caitlin Thomas." *Christian Science Monitor*, 10 Oct. 1957, p. 13.

"Book Event." *Human Events* 14, no. 43 (1957).

Chamberlain, John. "Ayn Rand's Political Parable and Thundering Melodrama." *New York Herald Tribune*, 6 Oct. 1957, sec. 6, p. 1+.

Chambers, Whittaker. "Big Sister Is Watching You." *National Review*, 28 Dec. 1957, pp. 594–96.

Donegan, Patricia. "A Point of View." *Commonweal* 67 (8 Nov. 1957): 155.

Hicks, Granville. "A Parable of Buried Talents." *New York Times Book Review*, 13 Oct. 1957, pp. 4–5.

Hughes, Riley. "Novels Reviewed." *Catholic World*, January 1958, p. 309.

Malcolm, Donald. "The New Rand Atlas." *The New Yorker*, 26 Oct. 1957, a019194–96.

McLaughlin, Richard. "The Lady Has a Message. . . . " *The American Mercury*, January 1958, pp. 144–46.

"No Walls Will Fall." *Newsweek*, 14 Oct. 1957, pp. 130–32.

Rolo, Charles. "Comes the Revolution." *Atlantic Monthly*, November 1957, pp. 249–50.
"The Solid-Gold Dollar Sign." *Time*, 14 Oct. 1957, p. 128.
Vidal, Gore. "Comment." *Esquire*, July 1961, pp. 24–27.
Woodward, Helen Beal. "Non-Stop Daydream." *Saturday Review*, 12 Oct. 1957, p. 25.

The Fountainhead: The Book

Derleth, August. Review. *Book Week*, 13 June 1943, p. 4.
Hirsch, Felix E. Review. *Library Journal*, 15 April 1943, p. 328.
Pruette, Lorine. "Battle against Evil." *New York Times Book Review*, 16 May 1943, p. 7 +.
Rothman, N. L. "H. Roark, Architect." *Saturday Review of Literature*, 29 May 1943, pp. 30–31.
Trilling, Diana. "Fiction in Review." *The Nation*, 12 June 1943, p. 843.

The Fountainhead: The Film

Crowther, Bosley. "Gary Cooper Plays an Idealistic Architect in Film Version of 'The Fountainhead.' " *New York Times*, 9 July 1949, p. 8, col. 5.
———. "In a Glass House." *New York Times*, 17 July 1949, sec. 2, p. 1.
McCarten, John. Review. *The New Yorker*, 16 July 1949, pp. 46–47.
Review. *Good Housekeeping*, 1 July 1949, p. 200.
Review. *Newsweek*, 25 July 1949, p. 76.
Review. *Time*, 11 July 1949, p. 95.

Night of January 16th

Atkinson, Brooks. Review. *New York Times*, 17 Sept. 1935, p. 26, col. 4.
Barnes, Clive. " 'Penthouse Legend,' A Courtroom Drama." *New York Times*, 23 Feb. 1973, p. 20, col. 1.
"Blind Jury Finds a Slayer Guilty." *New York Times*, 16 Dec. 1935, p. 22, col. 5.
"Play Uses Audience in Jury Box on Stage." *New York Times*, 10 Sept. 1935, p. 26, col. 1.

The Unconquered

Hartung, Philip T. "The Stage & Screen." *The Commonweal* 1 (March 1940): 412.

We the Living

Belitt, Ben. "The Red and the White." *The Nation*, 22 April 1936, pp. 522–24.
Cannon, Lee E. "The Quick and the Dead." *The Christian Century*, 1 July 1936, p. 941.
Straus, Harold. "Soviet Triangle." *New York Times Book Review*, 19 April 1936, p. 7.

Reviews of Rand's Nonfiction

Capitalism: The Unknown Ideal

Gillett, Elizabeth. "Other Books." *The Freeman* 17, no. 3 (March 1967): 189–90.
O'Shea, Daniel G. *American*, 21 Jan. 1967, pp. 118–20.
Review. *Christian Century*, 23 Nov. 1966, p. 1449.
Tracy, Honor. "Here We Go Gathering Nuts." *New Republic*, 10 Dec. 1966, p. 27–28.
Van Derhoof, Jack. Review. *Library Journal*, 1 Dec. 1966, p. 5984.

For the New Intellectual

Browning, Norma Lee. "Limping Crusade for Intellectualism." *Chicago Sunday Tribune*, 19 July 1961, sec. 6, p. 5.
Caritas, Sister M., C.H.M. Review. *Social Justice Review*, May 1965, p. 69.
Donahugh, Robert H. Review. *Library Journal*, 1 May 1961, p. 1781.
Hook, Sidney. "Each Man for Himself." *New York Times Book Review*, 9 April 1961, pp. 3, 28.
The Journal of Family Welfare 8, no. 1 (1961): 50–51.
Kirkus Service Reviews, 15 Dec. 1960, pp. 1065–66.
Rosenblum, Joel. "The Ends and Means of Ayn Rand." *New Republic*, 24 April 1961, pp. 28–29.

Introduction to Objectivist Epistemology

Bynagle, Hans. Review. *Library Journal*, 1 May 1979, p. 1062.
O'Neill, William F. Review. *Teaching Philosophy* 3, no. 4 (Fall 1980): 511–16.

Philosophy: Who Needs It?

Davis, L. J. "Ayn Rand's Last Shrug." *Washington Post*, 12 Dec. 1982, p. 7.
Den Uyl, Douglas. "Rand's Last Words." *Reason*, May 1983, pp. 71–74.

The Virtue of Selfishness

Brodie, Janis M. "Summaries and Comments." *Review of Metaphysics*, June 1967, p. 729.
Choice 2 (April 1965): 100.
Colimore, Vincent J. Review. *Best Sellers*, 1 Jan. 1966, pp. 386–87.
Kirkus Service Reviews, October 1965, p. 1060.
Loughan, Thomas. *American*, 5 Feb. 1966, p. 208.

Reference Articles and Obituaries

American Authors and Books (New York: Crown Publishing, 1962 ed.), p. 603.
American Novelists of Today (Westport, Conn.: Greenwood Press, 1951 ed.), p. 350.
"Ayn Rand, 'Fountainhead' Author, Dies." *New York Times*, 8 March 1982, p. 6.

"Ayn Rand, R.I.P." *Reason*, May 1982, p. 13.

Bryant, Jerry H. *The Open Decision: The Contemporary American Novel and Its Intellectual Background*, pp. 169–71. New York: The Free Press, 1970.

Buckley, William F. "On the Right: Ayn Rand Rip." *National Review*, 2 April 1982, pp. 380–81.

Cassell's Encyclopedia of World Literature (New York: Morrow & Co., 1973).

Childs, Roy A., Jr. "Ayn Rand 1905–1982." *Inquiry*, 26 April 1982, pp. 33–34.

Chira, Susan. "Tributes to Ayn Rand Stress Wide Influence of Her Work." *New York Times*, 10 March 1982, p. 3.

Contemporary Authors (Detroit: Gale Research Co., 1st ed., 1975), vols. 13–16, pp. 654–56.

Contemporary Literary Criticism (Detroit: Gale Research Co., 1975), pp. 423–24.

Contemporary Novelists (New York: St. Martin's Press, 2d ed., 1976), pp. 1139–41.

Gladstein, Mimi. "Ayn Rand." In *American Women Writers* 3 (1981): 438–39. Paperback vol. 2, pp. 167–68.

———. "Ayn Rand." In *Notable Women In the American Theatre* (forthcoming from University Publications of America, Inc.).

A Handbook of American Literature (New York: Crane, Russak & Co., 1975), p. 407.

"Libertarians Mourn Rand's Death." *Frontlines* 4, no. 7 (April 1982): 1, 3.

McDowell, Edwin. "Ayn Rand: Novelist with a Message." *New York Times*, 9 March 1982, p. 24.

"Obituary Notes." *Publishers Weekly*, 19 March 1982, p. 24.

Oxford Companion to American Literature (New York: Oxford University Press, 4th ed., 1965), p. 694.

Penguin Companion to American Literature (New York: McGraw-Hill, 1971), p. 213.

Political Profiles: The Eisenhower Years (New York: Facts on File, 1977), pp. 493–94.

The Reader's Encyclopedia (New York: T. Y. Crowell Co., 2d ed,. 1968), p. 840.

The Reader's Encyclopedia of American Literature (New York: T. Y. Crowell Co.), p. 937.

Saxon, Wolfgang, "Writer Ayn Rand Dies at 77." *Los Angeles Herald Examiner*, 7 March 1982, p. A–4, col. 2.

Teachout, Terry. "Farewell, Dagny Taggart." *National Review*, 14 May 1982, pp. 566–67.

Twentieth Century Authors: First Supplement (New York: Wilson, 1955), pp. 811–12.

200 Contemporary Authors (Detroit: Gale Research Co., 1969), pp. 225–27.

Webster's New World Companion to English and American Literature (New York: World Publishing, 1973), pp. 557–58.

Who's Who in 20th Century Literature (New York: Holt, Rinehart), p. 301.

Writer's Directory (Chicago: St. James Press, 1976–78), p. 874.

Letters

Branden, Barbara. "In Answer to Ayn Rand." Mailing to subscribers to *The Objectivist*, 16 Oct. 1968, pp. 7–12.

Branden, Nathaniel. "In Answer to Ayn Rand." Mailing to subscribers to *The Objectivist*, 16 Oct. 1968, pp. 1–6.

Brandon [sic], Barbara, et al. Letters to the Editor. "Atlas Shrugged." *New York Times*, 3 Nov. 1957, sec. 7, p. 46. (Barbara Branden, Dorothy Callman, and Allan Greenspan remonstrate against Granville Hicks' review of *Atlas Shrugged*.)

Brodsky, Allyn B., et al. Letters to the Editor. "The Rand Phenomenon." *New York Times Book Review*, 9 June 1968, p. 32. (Nora Ephron's 25th anniversary article on *The Fountainhead* elicited twelve letters.)

Gunkel, Patrick. Letter. "Mr. Reagan's Choice for Vice-President." *New York Times*, 1 Aug. 1976, sec. 4, p. 14, col. 3.

Holton, James E. (Archivist, Lewis and Clark College). Letter to Mimi R. Gladstein detailing Rand's visit on that campus, 6 Aug. 1982.

Moffat, Gertrude M. Letter to Editor. *New York Times*, 9 Oct. 1935, p. 22, col. 6.

Peikoff, Leonard. Letter to Editor. "Atlas Shrieked." *Esquire*, October 1961, pp. 14, 20.

University Studies of Rand

Davisson, Gary. "Ayn Rand's Objectivist Philosophy, Psychology, and Psychotherapy Implications for Therapy." *DAI* 35-A (June 1975), 7646A (Florida State University).

Lawson, David Clifton. "Ayn Rand: Her Systematic Appraisal of the Problems and Challenges Confronting Modern Man." MA thesis. University of Texas at El Paso, 1969.

Nighan, Raymond Andrew, Jr. "Ayn Rand's Concept of the Educated Man." *DAI* 35-A (August 1974), 859A (Loyola University of Chicago).

Vantrease, Brenda Riehman. "The Heroic Ideal: Three Views." *DAI* 41 (1980), 2106A (Middle Tennessee State University). (DeFoe, Bronte, Rand).

Other Materials

Branden, Barbara. "Who Is Ayn Rand?" Future of Freedom Conference, Long Beach, California, 2 Oct. 1982. Speech.

———. "Ayn Rand: The Charisma of Reason." Future of Freedom Conference, Long Beach, California, 23 Oct. 1983. Speech.

Branden, Nathaniel. *The Benefits and Hazards of the Philosophy of Ayn Rand: A Personal Statement*." Biocentric Institute, 1982. *Cassette tape*.

———. *The Basic Principles of Objectivism*. Audio-Forum. Set of 20 cassettes.

Greenberg, Sid. *Ayn Rand and Alienation: The Platonic Idealism of the OBJECTIVIST ETHICS and a Rational Alternative*. San Francisco: Sid Greenberg, 1977.

Nichols, Rosalie. *Confessions of a Randian Cultist: An Open Letter to Ayn*

Rand Regarding the Branden Interview. Brian Eenigenburg Publisher, 1972.

Peikoff, Leonard. *Ford Hall Forum Tribute.* Introductory remarks, recollections of Rand's final weeks, his delivery of her scheduled lecture. April 1982. Cassette tape.

————. *Modern Philosophy: Kant to the Present.* Taped course.

————. *The Philosophy of Objectivism.* Taped course.

————. *Understanding Objectivism.* Taped course.

————. *A Study Guide to the Ethics of Objectivism.* Revised by Leonard Peikoff and David Kelley. Palo Alto Book Service, 1977. Pamphlet.

PART III: WORKS THAT REFER TO RAND

Representative Articles and Books Which Include References to Rand and Her Ideas

Andelman, David A. "Aggressive Leader for Australia: John Malcolm Fraser." *New York Times,* 15 Dec. 1975, p. 22, col. 4.

Arnoldsen, Larry M. "Reading Made Necessary, Naturally!" *Journal of Reading* 25, no. 6 (March 1982): 538–42.

Axthelm, Pete. "Why It Went Wrong." *Newsweek,* 1 Nov. 1982, p. 38.

Barry, Norman P. "The New Liberalism." *British Journal of Political Science* 13, pt. 1 (January 1983): 99–123.

Beck, Clive. "Utterances Which Incorporate a Value Statement." *American Philosophical Quarterly* 4, no. 4 (October 1967): 291–99.

Branden, Nathaniel. "Break Free! An Interview with Nathaniel Branden." *Reason* (October 1971): 4–19.

————. "Rational Egoism: A Reply to Professor Emmons." *Personalist* 51 (Spring 1970): 196–211.

————. "Rational Egoism: Part II." *Personalist* 51 (Summer 1970): 305–14.

Cerf, Bennett. *At Random,* pp. 249–53. New York: Random House, 1977.

Chamberlain, John. "Edith Efron's Murderous Adding Machine." *National Review,* 5 Nov. 1971, pp. 1225–26, 1253.

————. *A Life with the Printed Word.* Chicago: Regnery Gateway, 1982.

Childs, Roy A. "Professor Kroy on Contract and Freedom: Comment." *Journal of Libertarian Studies* 1 (Summer 1977): 215–16.

Den Uyl, Douglas. "Ethical Egoism and Gewirth's PCC." *Personalist* 56 (Autumn 1975): 432–47.

Dickinson, Dan. "Dante Plays Prometheus." Review of *Catching Fire* by Kay Nolte Smith. *Reason* 15, no. 3, pp. 64–65.

Dwyer, William. "The Argument against 'An Objective Standard of Value.'" *The Personalist* 55 (Spring 1974): 165–81.

Ellis, Albert. "Psychotherapy and Atheistic Values: A Response to A. E. Bergin's 'Psychotherapy and Religious Values.'" *Journal of Consulting and Clinical Psychology* 48, no. 5 (1980): 635–39.

————. "Science, Religiosity, and Rational Emotive Psychology." *Psychotherapy: Theory, Research and Practice* 18, no. 2 (Summer 1981): 155–58.

Evers, Williamson M. "Social Contract: A Critique." *Journal of Libertarian Studies* 1 (Summer 1977): 185–94.

Farnham, Marynia. "The Pen and the Distaff." *The Saturday Review of Literature*, 22 Feb. 1947, pp. 7–8 +.

Farr, Finis. *O'Hara: A Biography*, pp. 262–63. Boston: Little, Brown and Company, 1973.

"Film Men Admit Activity by Reds: Hold It Is Foiled." *New York Times*, 21 Oct. 1947, pp. 1, 3.

"Fundamental Fountainhead." *Newsweek*, 5 Aug. 1974, p. 51.

"Goldwater People." *Look*, 3 Nov. 1964, p. 53 +.

Haydn, Hiram. *Words and Faces*, pp. 257–62. New York: Harcourt Brace Jovanovich, 1974.

Hill, Lewis E. and Robert L. Rouse. "The Sociology of Knowledge and the History of Economic Thought." *American Journal of Economics and Sociology* 36, no. 3 (July 1977): 299–309.

Hitchens, Christopher. "Downstairs, Upstairs." *New York Times*, 1 June 1975, sec. 6, pp. 16–31.

Holland, Thomas P. and Martha A. Cook. "Organizations and Values in Human Services." *Social Service Review* 57, no. 1 (March 1983): 59–77.

Kamm, Henry. "Scandinavia Tightens Hold on Welfare Costs." *New York Times*, 22 March 1974, p. 3.

Katz, Solomon H. "Biocultural Evolution and the Is/Ought Relationship." *Zygon* 15, no. 2 (June 1980): 155–68.

King, Billie Jean. "Interview." *Playboy*, 1976, pp. 55–70, 194–96.

Kroy, Moshe. "Political Freedom and Its Roots in Metaphysics." *Journal of Libertarian Studies* 1 (Summer 1977): 205–13.

Lefevre, Robert. "Professor Nelson on Government." *Personalist* 53 (Winter 1972): pp. 74–79.

Lehr, Stan and Louis Rosetto, Jr. "The New Right Credo—Libertarianism." *New York Times Magazine*, 10 Jan. 1971, pp. 24, 86.

Little, Graham R. "Social Models: Blueprints or Processes?" *Impact of Science on Society* 3, no. 4 (1981): 439–47.

Locke, Edwin A. "Critique of Bramel and Friend." *American Psychologist* 37, no. 7 (1982): 858–59.

Lugenbehl, Dale E. "The Argument for an Objective Standard of Value." *Personalist* 55 (Spring 1974): 155–64.

Machan, Tibor. "A Rationale for Human Rights." *Personalist* 52 (Spring 1971): 216–35.

———. "Some Recent Work in Human Rights Theory." *American Philosophical Quarterly* 17 (April 1980): 103–15.

———. "Wronging Rights." *Policy Review* 17 (Summer 1981): 37–58.

Mavrodes, George T. "Property." *Personalist* 53 (Summer 1972): 245–62.

McBride, William Leon. "Philosophy of Law." *Social Research* 47, no. 4 (1980): 775–88.

Nealis, Perry M. "Has Neurophysiology Resurrected the Platonic Soul?" *Psychological Reports* 35, no. 1 (1974): 611–19.

O'Hara, John. *Selected Letters of John O'Hara*, ed. Matthew J. Bruccoli, p. 413. New York: Random House, 1978.

Patai, Daphne. "British and American Utopias by Women (1836–1979): An Annotated Bibliography Part I." *Alternative Futures* 4, nos. 2–3 (1981): 184–206.

———. "When Women Rule: Defamiliarization in the Sex-Role Reversal Utopia." *Extrapolation* 23, no. 1 (1982): 56–69.

Poole, Ross. "Locke And the Bourgeois State." *Political Studies* 28, no. 2 (1980): 222–37.

Rafferty, George. "High School Favorites." *New York Times Book Review*, 27 Feb. 1966, pp. 14, 16.

Rasmussen, Douglas B. "A Critique of Rawls' Theory of Justice." *Personalist* 55 (Summer 1974): 303–18.

"The Return of Barbara Branden." *The Smart Set*, February 1982, pp. 2–4.

Thorne, F. C. "Essential Man in Society." *Journal of Clinical Psychology* 32, no. 2 (April 1976): pp. 507–8.

Rosen, Gerald R. "Can Alan Greenspan Win?" *Dun's Review* 104 (December 1974): 66–69.

Rush. *2112* Canada: Core Music Publishing, Phonogram, Inc., 1976.

Seeger, Murray. "Hope Still Found for Conservatism." *New York Times*, 5 Nov. 1964, p. 20, col. 7.

Spivak, Robert G. "Men behind Goldwater." *Look*, 11 March 1964, pp. 52–59.

Walton, Clarence C. "The Connected Vessels: Economics, Ethics and Society." *Review of Social Economy* 40, no. 3 (December 1982): pp. 251–90.

Wiesen, David L. "Population Obstacle." *Bulletin of the Atomic Scientists* 39, no. 1 (1983): 50–51.

Wilson, Ellen. "Judges, Jurists, and the Legal World of Ayn Rand." Review of *The Music of the Law* by Daniel Kornstein. *Wall Street Journal*, 10 March 1983, p. 26.

PART IV: IVAR KREUGER

Callender, Harold. "Exploring the Kreuger Legend." *New York Times Magazine*, 24 July 1932, pp. 1, 2, 13.

"Had Less Than $100 on His Arrival Here." *New York Times*, 13 March 1932, p. 22.

"Ivar Kreuger a Suicide." *New York Times*, 13 March 1932, pp. 1, col. 8; 22.

"Move to Protect Kreuger Holdings. . . ." *New York Times*, 7 May 1932, p. 23, col. 6.

"Sweden Authorizes Private Moratoria." *New York Times*, 13 March 1932, pp. 1, 22.

Index

ABOUT THE AUTHOR

MIMI REISEL GLADSTEIN is an Associate Professor at the University of Texas at El Paso where she has directed both the graduate and undergraduate programs in the Department of English. She has published articles on Steinbeck in the *Steinbeck Quarterly* and contributed chapters to *Steinbeck's Women: Essays in Criticism*. Her articles on Ayn Rand appear in *College English* and *American Women Writers*. She is also the author of articles in *The English Quarterly, Southwestern American Literature, Rocky Mountain Review*, and other scholarly journals.